The Power of Their Will

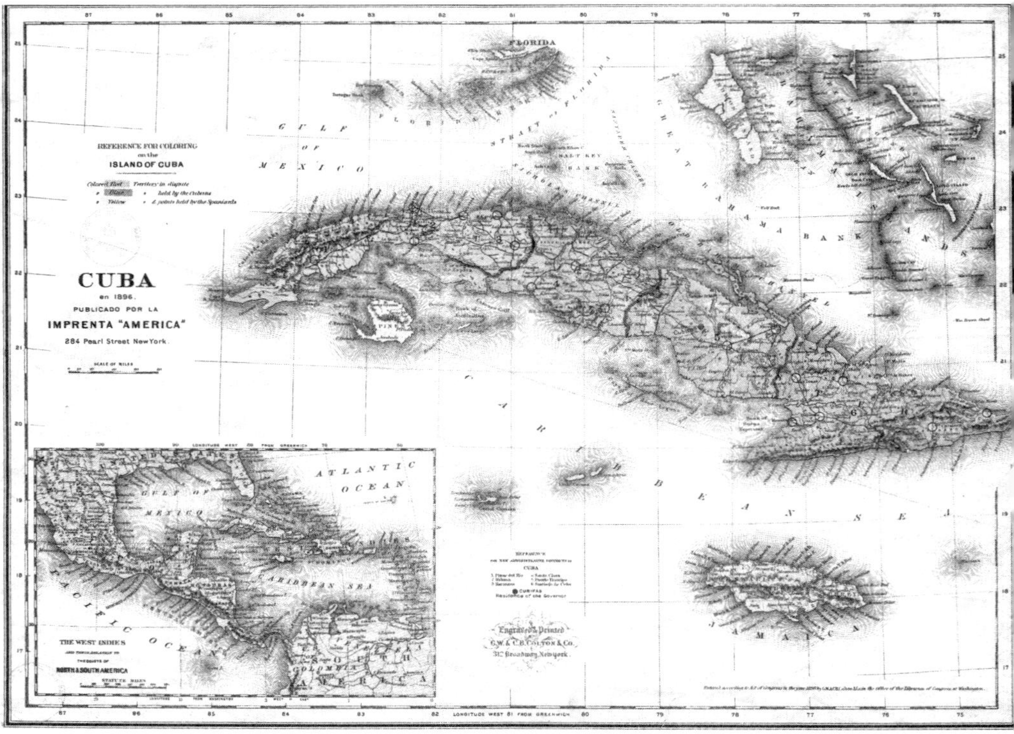

Frontispiece. Map of Cuba, 1896. New York: C. W. Colton, Imprenta América. BNJM, Map Collection.

The Power *of* Their Will

Slaveholding Women in Nineteenth-Century Cuba

TERESA PRADOS-TORREIRA

The University of Alabama Press   Tuscaloosa

The University of Alabama Press
Tuscaloosa, Alabama 35487-0380
uapress.ua.edu

Typeface: Minion Pro

Cover image: *El Quitrín*, by Frédéric Mialhe (1853); courtesy
of Biblioteca Nacional de Cuba José Martí
Cover design: Michele Myatt Quinn

Cataloging-in-Publication data is available from the Library of Congress.
ISBN: 978-0-8173-2079-9
E-ISBN: 978-0-8173-9335-9

To my dear friend Nancy Machado (1962–2020). As *subdirectora* of the José Martí National Library in Havana for many years, Nancy helped me, and hundreds of other scholars, find what we were looking for and what we didn't know was there.

Contents

Figures

Acknowledgments

I thank Wendi Schnaufer, senior acquisitions editor of the University of Alabama Press, for all her help and her positive spirit. It has been a pleasure to work with her. I also thank Joanna Jacobs, assistant managing editor at the press, and freelance copyeditor Lys Weiss, of Post Hoc Academic Publishing Services, for their helpful revisions and suggestions.

The members of the Windy City Writing Group—Benjamin Johnson, Andrae Marak, Margaret Power, Michael Staudenmaier, Ellen Walsh, and Neici Zeller—have been a model of collegiality. They read every chapter of my manuscript, identified the flaws, and encouraged me to move forward with this project.

In Santiago de Cuba, La Casa de Africa provided a wonderful platform for scholarly discussion with its annual conference. The archivist Maria Antonia Reina helped me find documents from the Archivo Provincial. My friend Damaris Torres Ellers, with whom I share many interests, assisted with information and guidance, as did several other members of the Universidad de Oriente History Department. Maciel Reyes, a promising young scholar, was also invaluable in helping me find information on coffee planters and their culture, as well as addressing every question I came up with. I remember fondly our many talks on nineteenth-century Cuban wills, a subject she masters. Nancy Machado, the *subdirectora* of the José Martí National Library in Havana, was a dear friend and the best possible ally a scholar could have. I benefited greatly from her knowledge of the library's collection and her understanding of Cuban bureaucracy. Her death, which occurred as I was proofreading these pages, is a devastating loss for both her friends and the academic community.

The staff of the Columbia College Chicago Library was a constant and reliable source of support.

I am also grateful to Steve Asma, Rojhat Avsar, Andrew Causey, Melanie Chambliss, Carmelo Esterrich, Rami Gabriel, Olga Goldenberg, Kate Hamerton, Robert Hanserd, Eliza Nichols, Michelle Yates, and the rest of my department at Columbia College Chicago, for being excellent colleagues.

I thank my friend María Ochoa for her insightful comments after reading the whole manuscript, and Allison English for keeping my body and mind in sync during the grueling process of writing the book. Namaste.

I was able to count on my siblings—Mayi, Dolores, Alfredo, Lourdes, Miguel, and Rocio—to help me translate obscure terms and much, much more.

I am particularly in debt to my husband, Joel Bleifuss, and to my sons, Adrian, Diego, and Eloy, for their help editing my manuscript, and for their love and support.

Introduction

THIS BOOK ADDRESSES a subject that historians of Cuba have largely neglected: the interactions and social dynamics between female slaveholders and the enslaved men, women, and children under their control in nineteenth-century Cuba. It examines the ways in which slave mistresses' authority both shaped and failed to shape the institution of slavery, and how their slaveholding role defined their own lives and the lives of their slaves.[1]

Cuba became a Spanish colony after Columbus landed on the island in 1492. From the beginning of the colonization period, Spain brought enslaved Africans to Cuba to work in the mines. This labor force was especially needed as Old-World diseases and the exploitation of the native population had genocidal consequences throughout the Americas. Slaves were also sent to work in the small sugar mills that proliferated throughout the island and in construction sites in growing towns. But the enslaved persons were most often domestic workers in private homes. In the late eighteenth century, after Saint Domingue's slave rebellion and the resulting collapse of its rich economy, Cuba transformed itself into a leading producer of sugar and coffee, two commodities that were becoming increasingly popular in Europe and the former American colonies. In 1789, encouraged by the Cuban planter class and in an attempt to emulate the British and French economic models, the Spanish crown put an end to what had been up until then a foreigners' monopoly on the slave trade, and opened the market in human beings to its subjects. Spanish entrepreneurs seized their opportunity, particularly after 1807, the year when Great Britain ended its participation in the slave trade and the British slave merchants sold their knowledge and establishments on the African coast to the Spanish newcomers.[2] Thus, in a tragic twist, Spain responded to the rise of abolitionist ideals and the subsequent decline of slavery throughout the Atlantic with a massive expansion of slave plantations in Cuba. Between the late 1790s and 1830, more than three hundred thousand Africans were captured, enslaved, and shipped to the island.[3] Dale Tomich has coined the term "second slavery" to describe the enormous growth of Cuba's (and Brazil's) plantation economy in the early nineteenth century, which resulted from the abolition of enslaved labor in so many other areas of the world.[4] Despite the agreements Spain signed with Britain in 1817 and then again in 1835 renouncing the slave trade, Africans continued to be brought by force to Cuba until 1867, if not longer. In 1817, the island's slave population was recorded at 199,000. By the 1840s it had increased to 436,000, with enslaved people and freed people of color making up 58 percent of the Cuban population, numbers that inspired fear among the white inhabitants. Between 1501 and 1866, more than 778,000 Africans were torn from their homelands and brought to work for the benefit of the Cuban slaveholding class.[5]

Current scholarship on the Caribbean highlights the importance of the region's slavery in the development of global capitalism. Coffee and, even more so, sugar production were intensely competitive businesses that aimed at maximum productivity and financial profit. Nineteenth-century Cuban planters can rightly be characterized as modern capitalists seeking profits in a highly competitive international market.[6] They were willing to experiment with crops and invest in the latest technical innovations. And although the Spanish empire had entered its twilight years, Spain was fully invested in protecting the great wealth that resulted from slave labor in its colonies.

Slave labor was phenomenally lucrative. It made members of the Cuban oligarchy fabulously wealthy, especially those who owned sugar mills, and turned the island into the most productive plantation society in the world. Enslaved people toiled on the vast sugar plantations in western and central Cuba, they labored on the eastern coffee plantations, and they did all sorts of domestic and manual jobs in every town throughout the island. The institution of slavery, alive until the 1880s, was the bedrock of the Cuban economy, defining its culture and society.

How significant was the institution of slavery for white women in Cuba? As colonial documents demonstrate, slaveholding women believed in, insisted on, petitioned for, and defended to local and colonial authorities their right to own slaves. Their lifestyle and economic status were at stake. Thousands of nineteenth-century Cuban women relied on the labor of enslaved people to maintain their social standing, whatever that happened to be. Large numbers of slaves provided wealthy plantation owners a luxurious existence, while a household with fewer slaves allowed middle-class women to lead a comfortable life. As for poorer women, the labor of their enslaved workers was what made the difference between getting by and living in poverty.

Female slaveholders lived in a patriarchal society that was framed by the

Spanish legal system. According to the Siete Partidas, Spain's most complete body of law (compiled by King Alfonso X in the thirteenth century, and ratified by the Nueva Recopilación in 1567 and the Novísima Recopilación in 1803), women were considered dependent on their fathers and husbands. However, women did have certain legal prerogatives, such as dowries, that provided them with a degree of independence. And if a woman was over the age of twenty-five and either single or a widow, she could make business decisions. But generally, Hispanic civil law, the law that ruled both Spain and the Spanish colonies, including Cuba, granted a husband the power to manage his wife's property and to represent her in any legal transaction.[7] Throughout the nineteenth century, Spain made multiple attempts to embrace liberal ideals, yet the weakness of its middle class, and a recalcitrant conservative segment of society including the powerful Catholic Church, made it difficult for the spirit of reform to succeed or last. Even during periods when liberal views prevailed, and not unlike the situation in other Western societies that were inspired by the ideals of the Enlightenment, women's standing remained unchanged. After Napoleon's invasion of Spain and the subsequent War of Independence, the Cortes de Cádiz produced the Constitution of 1812, a particularly advanced political document that included a call for universal suffrage. But nonetheless, women's rights were ignored. The same was true of the several liberal constitutions issued throughout the nineteenth century, including that of 1837. Even when women held property and were literate—two important conditions for suffrage during this century—they were not extended the status of citizens. Their exclusion was taken for granted.[8] Spanish liberals viewed a married woman as a caretaker; her role was not to participate in the marketplace but to create a harmonious home environment where her husband could retreat after a hard day's work and where her children could grow up in safety. It is undeniable that white women had less power, freedom, and mobility than their male counterparts.

But the law is one thing; another is the way a society actually operates. The civil restrictions imposed on women did not prevent them from being slaveholders. Their legal and political subordination notwithstanding, women could be property owners. Whether because they remained single all their lives, or because they continued to claim as their own what they had contributed to the marriage, or because they outlived their husbands, slave-owning women were not a rarity but a common occurrence. Nineteenth-century documents demonstrate that not only single women and widows but also married women had a strong sense of their status as owners of various types of property, including the enslaved men, women, and children they called their own. Married women who sat down to write their wills often specified which slaves were theirs and which ones belonged to their husbands. The same was true for women whose property was confiscated during the Ten Years' War, when their spouses were accused of political disloyalty. In their appeals to Spanish officials, they argued that the embargoed assets belonged to them and not to their husbands. The women's family and personal history as slaveholders trumped the legal limitations their society imposed on them. In her study of slaveholding women of the American South, Stephanie Jones-Rogers argues that historians have too often presented a "masculinized story of slavery's nineteenth-century expansion," by focusing exclusively on men and ignoring the role women played in that development.[9] The same can be stated for Cuban historiography, which has overlooked the fact that female slave owners enriched themselves and their families through the buying and selling of slaves. Women's active involvement in the institution of slavery was further strengthened by their cultural influence. Women presided over the domestic sphere and played a significant role in defining social mores. Their power and authority should not be minimized, no matter how subordinate their legal standing.

In this book, I explore slaveholding women's cultural influence, how Cuban expectations about female slaveholders and their appropriate behavior affected the lives of the enslaved populations over which they ruled, and how they helped maintain the status quo. Mistresses enforced punishment of rebellious slaves. But they also helped construct the illusion of slavery as a benevolent institution, a notion they also sought to instill in the slaves themselves, thus facilitating slaves' personal accommodations to their conditions. As Saidiya Hartman has written, "In every slave society, slave owners attempted to eradicate the slave's memory, that is, to erase all the evidence of an existence before slavery. This was as true in Africa as in the Americas. A slave without a past had no life to avenge."[10] Slaveholding women in Cuba played their parts in the process of erasing slaves' memories: Mistresses renamed them, insisted that they be baptized, often chose their clothing, and set norms of behavior for them. Households, in particular, but also plantations were ruled by cultural and social expectations to which enslaved people needed to adjust in order to survive and, occasionally, to thrive. In the domestic realm mistresses prescribed what was acceptable and expected. In this way, they played a role in the attempt to acculturate and assimilate their slaves: The assimilation process in Cuba resulted in the emergence of Cuban slaves as people with hybrid identities, African, European, and, ultimately, Cuban. On the one hand, this identity made enslaved people theoretically easier for slave owners to control because they understood Cuban rules and social codes; on the other hand, it posed a challenge to authority due to enslaved people's ease at navigating Cuban society.

The wide range of shapes and practices of nineteenth-century Cuban slavery serves as a reminder of how daunting it is for a historian to turn the complex, messy past into a clear narrative. Enslaved people worked in large sugar mills and on medium-sized coffee plantations, they lived in busy towns and in remote locations, and they worked as house servants, hired-out slaves, and semi-autonomous wage earners. The myriad ways in which enslaved workers experienced their bondage were paralleled in the variety of mistresses' experiences. The daily and intense interaction between slave-owning women and their domestic slaves in Havana, Santiago, or any other town was strikingly different from the influence that mistresses had on the slaves on plantations that were their own property, but which they rarely visited. Also significant is the contrast between wealthy women who owned sugar mills with hundreds of slaves and relatively poor women whose survival depended on hiring out one or more of their enslaved workers.

Women who, by themselves or jointly with their husbands, owned large plantations were members of the Creole elite that dominated the island's economy. Though of Spanish ancestry, Creoles were born in Cuba and identified with the island's culture and traditions, often competing for power with Spanish government officials and wealthy *peninsulares* (Spaniards born on the Spanish peninsula) who controlled banking and commercial interests, but also, at times, creating ties with them through marriage.[11] Members of the well-educated Creole middle class also invested in sugar and coffee plantations, finding a way to reconcile their enlightened values with the exploitation of slave labor. In the eastern provinces, many female slaveholders were French-speaking exiles from the Haitian revolution; others were American women from the southern states, whose families had moved to Cuba because the island offered what looked like an auspicious future for slave owners. In many urban centers, poor working women bought slaves with the purpose of renting them out. That group included a small number of Black women with full or partial West African backgrounds.

Slaveholding women's political views were as diverse as their social profiles, ranging from loyal support of Spain's colonial rule to rebellious opposition to it. Despite their many differences, the subjects I examine had two important things in common: they were women, and they legally owned another human being. That ownership gave them power, if in a different degree to that wielded by their male counterparts.

The term "mistress" has had multiple meanings throughout history. In contemporary culture the word acquired a sexual connotation, as it describes a woman in an illicit relationship, often with a married man. This meaning is at odds with nineteenth-century usage. Stephanie E. Jones-Rogers has pointed out that when applied to slave-owning women of the American South, the term implied the assumed dependency and vulnerability of the gentle southern white lady, while in a broader context, the term referred to women who governed over other people's lives—in other words, the female equivalent of "master."[12] In Spanish, there were three main terms used to refer to a slave-owning woman: *hacendada*, *ama*, and *señora*. "Mistress," as in someone who had power, is, in my opinion, one of the appropriate translations for those words because it captures the idea of having power to rule, just as the masters did.

Building on other scholarship on Caribbean and American slavery, this book explores the economic, social, and emotional implications of the relationship between female slaveholders and their slaves. Within the uneven power structure that framed their existence, a complex human interaction developed. Love and hate, indifference, jealousy, and other emotions characterized mistress-slave interactions, emotions that often are hard to trace in the documentary record, but that cannot be ignored because they are crucial to understanding that human relationship. Scholarship on slavery is becoming increasingly rich and nuanced as it moves beyond stiff dichotomies. Today's historians are freer than those in the past to reflect slaves' acceptance of their masters' and mistresses' power and their rejection of and resistance to it, and to examine how female slaveholders influenced their slaves and how they failed in their attempts to do so. As Stephanie Camp suggests, "Some scholars of slavery now consciously explore the contradictory and paradoxical qualities in bondspeople's lives: for instance, the ways in which they were both agents and subjects, persons and property, and people who resisted and accommodated—sometimes in one and the same act."[13]

My sources include government documents, literary fiction, newspaper articles, foreign travelers' accounts, women's wills, and visual images, including engravings. I have consulted provincial and national archives in Cuba, national archives in Spain, and a wide range of libraries in the United States. Despite the wealth of sources, I am aware that my narrative, far from being a complete picture of my topic, is a fragmented one. Historical narratives are conditioned by multiple elements: time, luck, the historian's intuition and skill, access to the archives, and the material the archive provides. Commenting on Haiti's historical records, Michel-Rolph Trouillot wrote that "historians alone do not set the narrative framework into which their stories fit. Most often, someone else has already entered the scene and set the cycle of silences."[14] In this case, the cycle of silences involves a combination of factors: The illiteracy of a large percentage of nineteenth-century Cuban women, even those who were members of the middle class, makes it harder to capture their voices. Certain topics, like the sexual rivalry between white and Black women, were considered taboo and addressed extensively in fiction but not in letters or other documents penned by those affected directly by them. The same can be said for the enslaved population: only one narrative exists written by a Cuban slave during the nineteenth century, and only half of that has been found. Other factors contributing to the silence on the topic of Cuban slave mistresses have to do with the view that they were irrelevant. Women's lack of political power led historians to assume that women had little influence in shaping the institution of slavery. Nationalism or political interests have also played a role. While Cuban, British, and American scholars have produced a rich historiography on Cuban slavery, for a long time that subject was a blind spot for Spanish historians who, as José Antonio Piqueras has pointed out, preferred to ignore this uncomfortable past. There is, however, a growing body of work on this topic.[15]

The goal of my narrative is to contribute to the understanding of slavery in nineteenth-century Cuba and how slaveholding women were an integral part of that institution. While focusing on slaveholding women, I hope also to shed light on the lives of slaves. Whenever possible, I provide their names as a way also to honor their past, their faint traces, in a modest attempt to recapture their individuality. As I wrote this book, I kept reminding myself to heed Vincent Brown's call to treat slavery as a predicament and not a condition.[16]

Chapter 1, "Female Slaveholders in Havana, Santiago, and Other Towns," explores the interaction between white mistresses—wealthy, middle-class, and lower-middle-class—and their slaves in an urban setting, and how they tried to shape and control slaves' lives legally, physically, and emotionally. An analysis of advertisements of slaves for sale or rent provides insight into the jobs enslaved domestic workers performed for their mistresses.

Chapter 2, "Visiting the Sugar Mill," follows a wealthy mistress as she pays a visit to her property in the country. I examine the consequences that the slaveholding woman's brief but significant visits had on the people over whom she ruled. What did each constituency expect to get out of that transitory interaction? How did the slaveholder perform during those encounters, and what opportunities did the meetings provide to cement or undermine her authority?

Chapter 3, "Coffee Plantation Mistresses," examines the idiosyncrasies of being the mistress of a coffee plantation and more particularly looks into the lives of women of French descent who settled on the eastern part of the island. Unlike sugar mills, coffee plantations tended to double as the residence of their owners.

Chapter 4, "'I Bequeath': Slaveholding Women's Wills," discusses how wills gave nineteenth-century Cuban women rare instances of legal power and a chance to reshape the fortunes of those around them, including their slaves. The documents provide us with the opportunity to hear the women's voices, even when they were illiterate, and capture, through a system of reward and punishment, both the personal and impersonal connections between mistresses and the enslaved.

Chapter 5, "*Amas* and the Ten Years' War," analyzes the fate of slaveholding women, mostly in Camaguey and surrounding areas, during the Ten Years' War. After the first major challenge to Spain's rule in Cuba, colonial authorities punished those disloyal to the government by confiscating their property, including their slaves. The consequences of that policy reveal the crucial economic role that slavery played in mistresses' and their families' survival.

Finding the right balance between highlighting slaveholding women's accountability for their role as owners of other people's lives, and at the same time acknowledging the limitations to their power, was challenging. Undoubtedly these women lived in a patriarchal society, their actions constrained by a legal framework that assigned them a subordinate role. It is also evident that white women played an important part in the survival of the institution of slavery in Cuba. Complexity and contradiction are two of the recurring themes in this story.

1

Female Slaveholders in Havana, Santiago, and Other Towns

WEALTHY SLAVEHOLDING WOMEN in Havana, Santiago, and other towns lived in comfortable, spacious homes. Entrance to their houses was through a gated courtyard that opened onto the first floor. Enslaved men, women, and children could be seen here, occupied in all the many productive tasks that were required in the quasi-self-sufficient households of the time: cleaning, making clothes, repairing shoes, and cooking the meals the masters would eat in an elegant dining room, also on this floor. A staircase led to an upstairs gallery around the courtyard and to the family's private area, the bedrooms and the large living room. Wardrobes, beds, and tables made of Cuban mahogany furnished the homes where the women spent much of their time. As captured by American artist Samuel Hazard in his sketches of domestic scenes, there were plenty of chairs and sofas to rest on and to receive their frequent visitors (figure 1.1). Framed color prints on the walls, dishes and ornaments of porcelain and cut glass gave the domestic space an elegant air. Cuban writer Cirilo Villaverde, author of *Cecilia Valdés* (a novel he began in 1833 and finished in 1882), captured the island's nineteenth-century white society with photographic realism. He wrote, "Everything exuded an air of cleanliness, tidiness and luxury."[1]

Foreign visitors to the island were remorseless in their depiction of wealthy women, whose lives they described as empty and their personalities as superficial. Mary Gardner Lowell, a resident of Lowell, Massachusetts, who visited Cuba in 1831 and 1832, accused Cuban ladies of doing nothing: "The greater part of the Spanish ladies do nothing but play upon the piano or harp, dance and dress."[2] It can be argued that her views were colored by her Puritan background, yet they were not much different from other foreigners' accounts. In 1844, the British artist Walter Goodman visited Cuba and left

Figure 1.1. *Saloon of Cuban Dwellings*, in Samuel Hazard, *Cuba with Pen and Pencil* (1871), 179.

an insightful record of the island's society, his observations re-creating the hospitable world of the Cuban slaveholding classes. Goodman's description of doña Mercedes, his hostess in Santiago de Cuba, confirmed a cultural stereotype that women were idle. He conjured up the portrait of a mistress and her domain: an ample and comfortable residence where the family received guests at all hours, the home always open to friends for an impromptu *tertulia* (social gathering). Characterizing doña Mercedes as a generous, kind woman, Goodman noted that her day was spent in leisure, her duties confined to overseeing the work of the slaves who were the ones responsible for performing all domestic tasks.[3] She and her daughters attended church in the morning, interspersing their prayers with quick glances to check their neighbors' clothes. They then went shopping along the city's main streets and paid visits to friends. After lunch and a siesta, the women dressed up and continued their vacuous lives. Throughout the evening they promenaded with other members of the city's distinguished families, listened to military bands, attended the theater, danced at the Filarmónica, and paraded by carriage on the *paseos* (boulevards), which were strictly segregated by race.[4]

James W. Steele, who was the American consul in Matanzas during the Ten Years' War, described the lives of typical Cuban ladies as "a great deal of rocking-chair and not much thrift."[5] Accusing such ladies of insipidity and backwardness, he wrote: "She does not know anything about cooperative kitchens, or the Sorosis, or her inalienable right to serve on committees, edit newspapers and lecture. There never was a woman's rights convention in this happy land, or a Dorcas society, or even a crusade."[6] In the opinion of many foreign observers, Cuban women of the comfortable classes were more determined than their husbands and fathers to maintain the island's rigid social hierarchy, as it was often the men's wives and daughters who refused to open up their gatherings to families of even a slightly lower social standing. The Spaniard Jacinto Salas y Quiroga, who visited Cuba in 1840, pointed out that women clung onto their respective rung of the social ladder because there was "a misplaced sense of pride among the ladies of the privileged classes that prevented sociability and interaction."[7] According to Salas y Quiroga, the result was a stifled and formal social life. The traveler J. B. Rosamond de Beauvallon, who came from the island of Guadeloupe, shared this opinion. He argued that while their male relatives were willing to socialize across classes, the women insisted on preserving the exclusivity of their circles and "remained immutable in their corresponding positions."[8]

It is often the case that travelers' accounts are based on an incomplete picture of the cultures they briefly encounter. Was the foreigners' critique of Cuban women fair or unfair, accurate or inaccurate? What the judgment lacked, in this case, was social context: Beauvallon and other critics failed to mention that nineteenth-century Cuban men had little to lose by occasionally breaking social barriers, while women faced the danger of damaged reputations. Men's lives were characterized by a flexibility and freedom that their female relatives lacked. White men received no penalty for occasionally flirting or having sex with women across social or racial lines. The vulnerable position women found themselves in made them especially intolerant and desirous of policing those boundaries men were so willing to cross, if only temporarily. And police them they did. Hippolyte Piron, a French Creole born in Santiago, found wealthy white women particularly antidemocratic and thought that they were more concerned with guarding a separation of racial lines than white men were. Piron's parents were among the many Saint Domingue residents who, following the revolution, had immigrated to Santiago and become successful coffee plantation owners. Their prosperity and their children's light skin had allowed the Piron family to shed their identity as *mulatos* (mixed race) and to "pass" as white. Like many members of the Santiago elite, they sent their children to study in Europe. In 1859, at the age of thirty-five, after spending years in France, Piron returned to Cuba and left a record of his impressions of an island and a society that were both familiar and foreign to him. Like many other nineteenth-century travelers, he was struck by the contrast between the comfortable classes' luminous social life and the slaves' harsh living conditions. His mixed-race background made him particularly attentive to the racial tension beneath the slaveholder-slave interaction. During his stay in Santiago, Piron observed numerous slaveholding families. His account of their habits and customs includes rich descriptions of the leisurely urban life enjoyed by the wives and mothers of the slaveholding class. He commented on how seldom the women walked and how instead they relied on carriages to take them to *paseos* for a promenade, or to concerts and dances. Piron praised the women's beauty and fashionable style, the splendor of their jewelry, their harmonious speech and languid movements.[9] But he also accused them of being fiercely preoccupied with maintaining racial boundaries, as illustrated by a story that many people in Santiago were familiar with in his day. On a Sunday evening, a beautiful and affluent lady, considered of mixed race, joined the usual line of carriages in the *paseo* la Alameda, where the well-to-do spent their time socializing, listening to music, showing off their elegant clothes, and parading their daughters of marriageable age. Once they realized she was there, one by one the other women left the *paseo* until the lady in question was left alone, prompting her to complain that she was treated like a leper (*pestilente*).[10]

Cuban women's education in the early nineteenth century was limited and unregulated. Girls were expected to follow their mothers' examples by learning behavioral norms, religious precepts, and basic feminine skills (such as sewing) at home. If girls were fortunate enough to have literate mothers, they would learn reading and writing from them. But, considering the high level of illiteracy among the Cuban female population, that was rarely the case. Affluent families often hired tutors who gave their girls lessons at home, usually until they reached puberty. Also popular among the wealthy was the practice of sending daughters to be educated at a convent, where they would receive thorough Catholic instruction and the necessary skills to become proper ladies—including, as María del Carmen Barcia points out, "how to watch and control their servants, be they enslaved or free."[11] As the decades went by, women's educational opportunities expanded with the growth of religious schools and small private academies where girls learned subjects that were considered appropriate for young ladies, such as grammar, penmanship, history, geography, music, drawing, and French.[12] By the 1840s there was a gradual opening of public schools for girls. The government-approved textbooks leaned toward heavy moralizing, reminding female pupils of the importance of being virtuous and modest, with more general information that would allow the students, once they became young women, to be competent wives and mothers.[13] As late as the mid-century, according to the 1862 Census, 65 percent of the white female population remained illiterate.[14]

It is clear, then, that nineteenth-century Cuba was a patriarchal society that offered few platforms for women to voice their social and political ideas. With their limited education and heavy influence from the Catholic Church, it is unsurprising that many women clung to traditional values, as so many travelers remarked. But—though this was hard to see for outsiders not attuned to the subtle signs of changing views—the reality was more complex. The foreigners simply failed to see the whole picture. Their comments about parasitic existences were directed at affluent women. Yet beyond the elite, women, especially the younger generations, were becoming active participants in the modernization of society that took place in the nineteenth century. As the winds of liberalism swept through Latin America, Cuban men and women were exposed to ideals that celebrated freedom and undermined tradition.[15] The changing political landscape was accompanied by the Cuban economic boom with its new emphasis on consumption. In *Intimations of Modernity* (2017), Louis Perez Jr. argues convincingly that, as consumers and members of civil society, women helped transform the island's cultural tenets. Particularly in urban centers, middle-class women embraced change and celebrated every new opportunity they had to contribute to the public sphere.[16] And just like their male counterparts, women were also becoming politically engaged and critical of the colonial status, as would be proven by their involvement in the wars against Spain in the second half of the century.[17]

But it is also true that Cuban society was filled with contradictions—the crucial one being the fact that the island's prosperity and modernization were built on the shoulders of an enslaved workforce. Before the 1860s, few white Cubans—male or female—raised their voices against slavery, which they took as a fact of life. Town dwellers, in particular, considered urban slavery benign and civilizing, especially when compared to the conditions found on plantations. Jobs that urban slaves performed were indeed less brutal than those done by plantation slaves, and their opportunities to expand their social networks, make their own money as hired workers, and ask for help if the masters mistreated them were slightly greater. Yet the constant personal interaction with their masters that domestic enslaved workers had to endure also made them vulnerable to all sorts of punishments and injustices. Foreign travelers tended to agree about the better treatment slaves experienced in the larger towns, but the most observant ones were not impressed by the urban slaves' conditions. Hippolyte Piron pointed out that urban slavery was not as devastating as that of rural areas, but he denounced it as cruel and dehumanizing nonetheless. "The surprising thing," Piron sarcastically observed when discussing the harsh lives the enslaved population endured, "is that their masters—their enemies and executioners—pretend candidly to earn their friendship. They often say with bitterness, as if their sentiments were hurt: 'The slaves do not love us in any way, they are mean, they'd like to harm us; it's an evil and damnable race.'"[18]

Walter Goodman, the aforementioned British artist, was struck by the differences between slave owners' privileged lives and their slaves' abject subjugation: Upon arriving on the island as the guest of a prominent Santiago family, he was treated to a lavish banquet and a beautiful scene. There were pretty ladies in light muslin dresses, gentlemen in white drill suits, a long table covered by snowy tablecloths, clean and shiny walls, resplendent sun coming through doors and windows—all these in stark contrast with the somber appearance of the slaves serving the delicious dishes.[19] Cirilo Villaverde also denounced the upper classes' opulent lifestyle in contrast to that of the enslaved population they controlled. Describing a typical dinner at Havana's Sociedad Filarmónica, the musical club where the town's elite, dressed in clothes as fashionable as those from Paris, socialized, he wrote, "Supper began between midnight and one in the morning, and consisted of cold turkey, Westphalian ham, cheese, excellent leg of lamb, braised shredded beef, candied fruit preserves, full-bodied wines from Spain and other countries abroad, rich chocolate, coffee, and fruits from every country that traded with the island of Cuba. And what was most noteworthy was that, with the splendor of the table rivaling its prodigal abundance, the dishes cost nothing but the effort of asking to be served them."[20] After one such night, the writer who, as an insider, knew this society well, has his fictional mistress, doña Rosa, wake up early in the morning to keep an eye on the work of the household's nine slaves, while she drank her *café con leche*. From that vantage, where she sat every day, she was able to watch slaves' activities: "whether the washerwomen were preparing the bleach for the laundry or the brazier with hot coal embers for the ironing; whether the seamstresses, instead of getting to work sewing the clothes for the slaves, were wasting their time chatting with other servants; whether the drivers were washing the carriages and greasing and cleaning the horses' harnesses; . . . whether Pío . . . was in the *zaguán* making women's shoes for the house servants and sometimes even for the mistress of the house, . . . finally, whether the cook . . . had gone at daybreak to the nearby market in the Plaza Vieja, to pick up vegetables and other provisions that he had been told to buy the night before."[21]

In *El Negro Francisco*, Antonio Zambrana's 1873 novel set in the 1860s, a main character, doña Josefina de Orellana, is described as one of the most distinguished ladies of Havana's society. Her opinion, in matters of etiquette, customs, and religious piety, holds social sway. Whatever she says and does is the accepted norm. Her elegant home in town is a symbol of Cuba's colonial oligarchy. The downstairs is the area where the servants work and live, with marble stairs leading up to the master's residence. A circular gallery provides a comfortable place to sit for the family, while also allowing the lady to keep an eye on slaves' activities. A widow, doña Josefina is in charge of the family's decisions. When the novel begins, she is gossiping with her son while checking the paper, and complaining about how difficult it is becoming to find good slaves to buy, a fact she blames on abolitionists. She proclaims, "Cuba without slaves would go bankrupt, they lived like animals in their land, ignorant of religion."[22] Like the fictional doña Josefina, Cuban slave owners scoured the daily papers looking for slaves. If evidence is needed of the prominent role women played in the institution of slavery, it can be found in how involved slaveholding women were in shaping the lives of their urban, domestic slaves. In her book about American slaveholding women, Stephanie Jones-Rogers has emphasized the significance of the domestic realm as a component of the marketplace. She writes: "The household became an extension of the slave market, and white women capitalized upon their access to both."[23] Cuban homes were also a site where transactions involving enslaved workers took place regularly, with mistresses actively involved in discussing prices, and in purchasing, selling, and hiring slaves.

By the early 1800s Cuba was experiencing a rapid transformation, and the enslaved population had become a valuable commodity in the island's booming market economy. While Havana counted some fifty thousand slaves in the late eighteenth century, the number had almost quadrupled by the early 1860s.[24] In other words, despite the official end of the slave trade and pressure from Britain, Cuba received greater numbers of African slaves in the early decades of the nineteenth century than ever before, and the enslaved men, women, and children contributed greatly to the financial well-being of the urban slaveholding class.

Slaveholders put up their slaves for sale for various reasons: In some cases, the family was moving abroad, or the children were grown and not as much domestic help was required. At times the reason was the considerable monetary reward of selling a skilled slave, or the convenience of disposing of one that was too young or too sick to contribute to the household. At others, mistresses were dissatisfied with their slaves' attitude or work, perhaps because they were not sufficiently docile or skillful. The slaves for sale could also be *bozales* (recently arrived Africans), though those, with an arduous process of acculturation ahead of them, tended to be sent, not to town houses, but to plantations. Every day, city newspapers published hundreds of notices advertising slaves for sale or for rent. The men, women, and children who were sold and bought for domestic work were closely overseen by their mistresses. It is logical to assume that mistresses would be the ones deciding whether their households needed to purchase a slave with a certain skill, or to replace and sell slaves with whom they were dissatisfied. They would be the ones approving the acquisition of slaves who would be integrated into their families' private sphere, and the ones determining what slaves' occupations should be. They would also be the ones molding the new slaves' behavior to make them fit the home rules and expectations.

Owning domestic slaves was a status symbol. "It is the ambition of the Spaniards to have as many slaves about the doors as possible and the opulent keep a great many simply for show," wrote Mary Gardner Lowell.[25] But more than anything else, owning domestic slaves made the life of slaveholding families comfortable, their households efficient. According to the 1830 census, Havana's white households counted between six and twenty-seven slaves, some doing domestic chores and others hired out.[26]

We do not know enough about the process of writing the advertisements for newspapers. Did mistresses dictate the ads? Did they write the ads themselves and then ask their husbands to have them published? Who made the decisions about whether to keep a mother and child together or to ignore that bond when buying and selling? Given women's prominent roles in households, it seems likely that behind every domestic slave bought and sold there was a mistress making the decision.

Newspaper advertisements give us a sense of the qualities that were valued when buying an enslaved person. Buyers sought men and women with specific domestic skills. Washing, cooking, ironing, and household cleaning were the abilities that mistresses expected of an enslaved woman worth her price. Knowing how to sew and embroider were additional selling points. Other desirable skills included knowing how to comb women's hair, nurse the sick, make women's clothes, care for children, and be a competent lady's personal maid (*servicio de la mano* or *a la mano*). All of these occupations, especially that of lady's maid, involved a close interaction with the mistress. That constant interaction, according to the traveler Rosamond de Beauvallon, who identified with the slaveholding class, made it difficult for white women to have private lives: their houses were always open, their slaves aware of their every move.[27] What was the interaction between housemaids and mistresses like in those close quarters? Given the uneven power relations, did slaves and mistresses ever get close? Could they be intimate? In her study of antebellum America, historian Sharony Green suggests an affirmative answer to these questions, finding proof that Black and white people, despite their unequal statuses, could have feelings for one another, their closeness the natural consequence of sharing the same abode. She writes: "Though intimacy and love are not always a consequence of sharing space (and a bed) with another human being, sharing space has real psychological consequences, some of them thoughtfully or unknowingly cultivated by one or both parties."[28] It is plausible that mistresses and slaves were able to develop a warm relationship. But given their unequal footing, it only makes sense to assume that intimacy, constantly inhabiting the same space, could also have the opposite effect, and lead to tension, resentment and hatred.[29] Referring to slaves of the American South, Stephanie Camp reminds us that enslaved people "lived multiple lives, some visible to their owners and to the archival record, some less visible. Side by side, public and hidden worlds co-existed . . . ; their black and white inhabitants shared space, agreed on its importance and clashed over its uses."[30] Enslaved people brought to work in a Cuban household must have faced the same kind of conflicted interests, as they attempted to live full lives while sharing a space with slaveholders and their families.

Purchasing an enslaved woman with her child, even if that meant paying a slightly higher price, could be a smart financial decision if the child was healthy and survived into adulthood (always an unforeseeable proposition, given the high rates of infant mortality). On July 1, 1840, *El Diario de la Habana* published the following ad: "A strong, humble, healthy woman, without flaws [*sin tachas*], good at washing, average at ironing, and really good at cooking certain dishes, for 400 pesos, tax free for the buyer, or for 600 pesos together with her five- or six-year-old daughter, very smart for whichever activity she is wanted or can also be exchanged for a good cook."[31] In other words, a mistress who agreed to buy a woman capable of performing multiple domestic tasks would also acquire a smart girl who could be trained to do a number of jobs or later sold for a profit. A few days later, the same paper ran this advertisement: "A good looking 20-year-old female slave, good at washing, ironing, and sewing, and an excellent lady's maid, with a two-year-old boy, healthy and without flaws for 500 pesos, no taxes, can also be sold by herself." In this case, if the two-year-old survived infancy, the owner would have gained another laborer who worked for free, and thus increased the value of her property.[32] In some cases, it was more convenient for mistresses simply to hire slaves, instead of buying them. Again, there were plenty of choices, as illustrated by this 1850 advertisement in Santiago's paper, *El Redactor*: "For rent, a slave washerwoman, ironer and cook, very well behaved for the amount of 10 pesos per hour on San Gerónimo Street number 75 for information."[33]

A special category of slave, and one for which mistresses undoubtedly would have been the ones making the purchasing decisions, was that of women who were bought or hired as wet nurses, "with or without child" as the ads sometimes put it, though the option of separating mother and child became less common by the 1840s.[34] In her study of slaveholding mistresses in the American South, Elizabeth Fox-Genovese argued that nursing one's own baby was not necessary to fulfill the ideal of motherhood.[35] The same was true for affluent Cuban mothers: aristocratic and upper-middle-class women felt no compulsion to breastfeed their children, a task that was an uncomfortable reminder of their sexuality. For Cuban upper-class women, appealing to female delicacy was enough to justify their transferring that responsibility to Black women, who were assumed to lack that quality. Multiple newspaper ads provided a solution: In 1835, the daily Havana paper *Noticiero y Lucero* offered an African-born woman (*negra de nación*), who had given birth fifteen days before, with or without her baby (*con cría o sin ella*).[36] In 1838, for example, the same paper advertised a young and strong woman, who had given birth two months earlier, but whose baby had died.[37] And in 1840, when perusing their paper, Havana slave owners could find for rent a wet nurse, described as humble, who had given birth two months earlier, with good and abundant milk.[38]

It is possible that in some cases the reason a mistress opted for selling a particular slave had to do with sexual rivalry, though this cannot be proven. As I will discuss in the following chapter, Cuban literature is filled with examples of mistresses sending a female slave to the family's plantation when she was suspected of having sex with the master. In a society where men juggled uneasily their patriarchal privileges and the Christian moral tenets, a young female slave could become a threatening presence in the household. No document has been found yet in which a real-life Cuban mistress discusses this matter—nothing comparable to the poignant comments Mary Chesnut left in her Civil War diary on how southern ladies felt about their husbands' infidelities. Chesnut wrote: "Like the patriarchs of old our men live all in one house with their wives and their concubines, and the mulattoes one sees in every family exactly resemble the white children—and every lady tells you who is the father of all the mulatto children in everybody's household, but those in her own home she seems to think drop from the clouds, or pretends so to think."[39] It is clear that, as Sharony Green points out when referring to the American South, married women seldom challenged their husbands, and even wives who became aware of their husbands' sexual relationships with slaves rarely got divorced. White women risked losing financial stability and good social standing.[40] But one thing a mistress could do when facing that predicament was to sell the offending slave.

When *Diario de la Habana* advertised "a young woman, about twenty-two, good as wet nurse, with her mulatto baby, with good and abundant milk, excellent cook and washer woman,"[41] one has to wonder what was the story behind the sale of a young female slave with a child fathered by a white man. Who was the child's father? Could he have been the master? A son in the family? Was that the reason the young woman was being sold? A similar question is raised by another ad: "A slave woman about twenty-three, nice presence, above average at basin washing and ironing, average at cooking, healthy and without vices, for 21 ounces [of gold, approximately 355 pesos], free of tax for the buyer, offered at this price to the buyer because she comes with a free [that is, nonenslaved] fourteen-month-old mulatto daughter."[42] In this case, it is likely that the white father had freed his child, a common request from enslaved mothers who had sexual relations with their masters or other free men in a position to buy the child's manumission.[43] The fact that in the mid-1800s, 86 percent of *mulatos* were free suggests that the practice of white men liberating the children they had with enslaved Black women was not uncommon.[44]

When it came to enslaved men, the domestic skills that owners valued included being a competent cook, shoemaker, and tailor, and being able to make either white women's clothes or slaves' clothes, as the following two ads from July 4, 1840, illustrate: "For sale: A young Black man, above average cook and shoemaker for women, and skilled at making clothes for the servants, very smart for everything, healthy and without vices for 500 pesos." "For rent, a seventeen-year-old, above-average cook, apprentice shoemaker for women's shoes."[45] A prestigious occupation for an enslaved man, and one that slave owners paid particular attention to because of its visibility, was that of coachman (*calesero*). In *Cecilia Valdés*, Cirilo Villaverde wrote that "as long as they were not on foot or paying a formal visit, two, and better yet three, young ladies could quite properly go all about the city, do their shopping, chat with the Spanish errand boys in the shops, and, on the nights when there were band concerts in the Plaza de Armas or on the Alameda de Paula, receive respects of their friends and the adoration of their lovers offered them from the footboard of their carriages."[46] The typical carriage sat three women, two of them comfortably reclining in the back seat and one, usually the youngest, in the middle seat, sitting straight. As the man conveying his owners from one place in the city to another in carriages called *quitrines* and *volantes*, but especially as the servant responsible for transporting the white women, the *calesero* was the family's public face. Seated on top of the open carriage, he wore an elaborate uniform that included the household livery, leather shoes with gold buckles, silver ornaments clasping his pants, a linen shirt, a black tie, top hat, and a silk cravat. The *calesero*'s impressive looks were meant to proclaim a slaveholder's economic power and social standing.[47] In an article included in *Tipos y costumbres de la Isla de*

Cuba (1881), the writer José E. Triay described the typical *calesero* as young, strong, and handsome, and particularly loyal to the young female family members. "He became the *girl*'s confidant. He brought her the letters from her suitor and carried her in the volante without the *old woman*'s knowledge . . . If the game was discovered, he could get sent to the sugar mill, and be discharged from his position, unless the girl's will was so powerful that he gained an amnesty before the terrible sentence was executed."[48]

Slaveholding women also liked to buy children who could help with certain domestic tasks and add prestige to the household. Newspaper offers praised the children's ability to entertain the family's youngsters, stated that they would make excellent ladies' servants and pages, and touted their general ability to perform whichever task the masters wanted to assign them (*a cuanto quieran aplicarlo*). A common responsibility for slave children was to carry a rug and a chair for their mistresses to kneel and sit in church. When visiting Santiago, Hippolyte Piron attended mass at the city's cathedral and noticed the presence of elegantly dressed ladies, "accompanied by a *negrito* or a *negrita*, carrying a seat, a rug and a prayer book." "The slave extended the rug carefully," wrote Piron, "positioned the chair, handed the book, and moved away with humility. The lady kneeled, murmured a prayer, fanned herself and looked around. As soon as her dark eyes recognized someone, she smiled to say hello. Women of various social classes intermingle, as long as they dress richly and are accompanied by the *negritos* carrying the chair and the rug."[49] American visitor Samuel Hazard left an enduring image of this practice in his drawing of a church in Santa Clara, where a pious lady kneels on a rug and prays in front of an altar, while the enslaved boy kneels on the floor behind her, his hand on her chair (figure 1.2). Young slaves were asked to perform many other tasks, including childcare, which must have been a heavy burden for the enslaved youths. "An eleven-year-old little mulatta, with a pretty figure, good for playing with children and whatever task the owner wants to assign her, healthy and without defects for 300 pesos," advertised *El Diario de la Habana* in 1840.[50] In 1849, *La Gaceta* offered "a fifteen- or sixteen-year-old boy, very skilled and humble and used to taking care of children."[51] A few months later the same paper announced for sale: "A very apt little black girl skilled at all domestic tasks and good for entertaining children being very affectionate for $6 a month, and another one for sale about ten years old who can sew and clean the house for 15 ounces free for the buyer, healthy and without flaws."[52] A decade later, though the offers were not as prevalent as in previous years, a mistress could still find advertisements for children: "For rent, a little mulatto, ten or eleven years old, good for whichever task is wanted," read an ad in *El Siglo. Diario Político, Económico, Literario y Mercantil*.[53]

Figure 1.2. *Church of Sta [Santa] Clara*, in Samuel Hazard, *Cuba with Pen and Pencil* (1871), 127.

Mistresses favored a certain racial type: on July 15, 1840, the *Diario de La Habana* included the following ad: “For sale, a young black boy, about nine years old, healthy and without defect, for whatever task wants to be assigned, price to be negotiated, and looking to buy a little mulatto boy not older than five or six years old.”[54] Why sell a healthy nine-year-old and buy a younger boy? Not knowing the full story, we can only speculate. It is clear that looks were important, and so was the color of the enslaved person; mixed-race and lighter skinned slaves were more sought after than darker ones, and beauty was a selling point. On November 21, 1849, Havana's *La Gaceta* published the following ad: “For sale, a little mulatta with straight hair [*de pelo*] appropriate for a girl.”[55] A few days later, the same paper posted this advertisement: “A light mulatto, straight hair [*de pelo*], good figure, twenty-one years old, looks white.”[56]

Juan Francisco Manzano's *Autobiography* is the only first-person narrative left by a Cuban slave during slavery, and it is particularly appropriate to this study because he was owned by two women, both of them members of the Creole aristocracy. His account narrates the ordeal of a young house slave and describes the effects his enslavement had on him.

Born around 1797 in Matanzas, Manzano enjoyed a happy early childhood. His first mistress, Beatriz de Justiz, marchioness de Santa Ana, treated him, in his words, "as a form of entertainment. They say she held me in her arms more than my mother . . . I grew up alongside my mistress without leaving her side except to sleep, for she never even traveled to the countryside without taking me along in the coach."[57] Playing with his mistress's grandchildren and pampered by his "mama," Manzano must have had a conflicted sense of identity. "On one occasion," he recounted, "my father shook me harshly for being quite unruly. My mistress found out and that was enough for her to refuse to see my father for several days until she restored him to her good graces at the behest of her confessor, . . . She did so only after making clear to him which parental rights were his and which hers as a slaveholder who assumed the role of a mother."[58]

When his mistress died, Manzano, who was twelve years old, was devastated. His new owner, the marchioness of Prado Ameno, assigned him the role of her personal page, and provided him with the fancy clothes pages wore, scarlet pants and a velvet vest. But her unstable, sadistic personality created a constant feeling of insecurity and fear in the young slave. His tasks included spending hours standing next to his mistress, while she played cards until midnight with her aristocratic friends, his elbows spread open to prevent anyone from crowding her space. If he fell asleep while performing his duties, he was sent to the stocks and whipped. He was expected to devote all his time to the marchioness, who had turned him, as he put it, into her lapdog. "One can say this because it was my duty to always follow her, except into her rooms, and I was to remain at the door keeping everyone out or calling whomever she requested, or demanding silence."[59] For a short time, he got a happy break when he was loaned out to live in Havana and then in Guanajuay with a younger master and his wife, both of whom treated him fairly. The young mistress "lavished me with every possible favor" and taught him how to sew women's garments.[60] But his old mistress requested him back, and his hellish life began again. He was by then a teenager who admired his powerful owner and was grateful when she was kind to him. "I loved her like a mother," he wrote, but her unpredictable cruelty had a confusing and devastating impact on him. Her punishments were horrific: she had him locked up for days in a coal cellar, ordered the *mayoral* (overseer) to give him hundreds of lashes, had his head shaved for minor offenses and misunderstandings, and sent him to labor in the sugar fields, a job he had no endurance for. On one occasion, when Manzano tried to get the small inheritance his mother, who had been freed, left for her children, the marchioness objected and argued that she was the "automatic heir" of her slaves. She also resented Manzano's attempt to get papers to find a new master, a common practice in Cuba, and made him feel guilty and undeserving of all her attentions.[61] By the time Manzano was about twenty years old (sometime between 1814 and 1817) he was able to escape and move to Havana, where he entered the service of several wealthy families, published poems in local papers, and befriended a group of white Creole reformers. This circle of intellectuals became interested in Manzano's life story and helped him to publish his autobiography, and eventually to gain his freedom in 1837. Once a freeman, he worked in various trades, and coped the best he could with chronic depression, a condition he endured until his death in Havana in 1854.

Health and good character were important characteristics that sellers never failed to mention when trying to sell or rent slaves. Masters and mistresses looked for slaves without physical defects or behavioral issues that made them difficult to manage. Mistresses wanted to be reassured that the slaves for sale were, above all, healthy, but also docile, affectionate, with good manners, faithful, and humble, as the following ad indicates: "Looking to buy a woman slave, general seamstress, without vices, who is not accustomed to going out on the streets."[62] A month later, the same paper advertised a slave for sale, one of whose selling points was the fact that she was not fond of socializing on the streets: "For sale a slave woman of irreproachable behavior, everyday cook, average at basin washing and ironing, knows how to sew, fillet, and marinate, gave birth a month ago, with her child, both of them very healthy, with good and abundant milk, not a friend of going out on the street, even though it is a custom in this one [street] to do so from time to time on holidays, she shows little or no interest in doing so."[63]

Reflecting the inevitable tension between slaveholders and slaves are the numerous ads in search of runaway slaves, a staple of daily papers. If recaptured, runaway slaves would be harder to sell. Who would want to buy an ungrateful troublemaker? A mistress in Havana placed an ad to try to find her slave Jose María, who was in his early twenties. The man had worked as a rented coachman and was described as being of average height, with a small sore on his ankle, dressed in a shirt and not very clean white pants, and wearing a wide-rim straw hat. The announcement promised a reward to whoever helped secure the slave and made responsible whoever hid him.[64] Similar ads could be found regularly. In 1857, a twenty-year-old man named Manuel almost escaped from his mistress, Havana resident Evelina Landos de Acosta, when he ran away, making it all the way to Santiago de Cuba. Three years later, however, she found out that he was working in that city as a coachman of rented carriages and demanded the help of the law getting him back. She assured the authorities that she was willing to pay for the corresponding expenses.[65] When runaway slaves were caught, they were sent to one of the city's *depósitos*, either a government official's private home or a public institution. The owners were notified, asked to collect them, and to pay for the expenses the municipality had incurred, an action that slaveholders did not always think worthwhile if the slaves were troublemakers. In 1854, a runaway slave called Santiago Macía, who had been caught and imprisoned, spent months doing forced labor while his mistress, a resident of Arcos de Canasí (a small town east of Havana) ignored the authorities' calls to pick him up and pay the appropriate fines.[66]

A crucial factor to determine the price of individual slaves was the number of slaves available generally. With the official end of the slave trade in 1817, slave owners feared it would become more challenging to fulfill their need for enslaved labor. Yet, though the trade was illegal, hundreds of thousands of Africans continued to be brought by force to Cuba throughout the early 1800s. The Cuban planter class had nervously watched the antislavery position of Spanish liberalism during the constitutional period of 1810–14, and then again in 1820–23, but the restoration of an absolutist monarchy in 1823 left the oligarchy at ease and strengthened the good feelings between the slaveholding group and Ferdinand VII. And even after the monarch's death and the return of a constitutional framework, the numbers of Africans brought by force to Cuba increased, despite Spain endorsing a new agreement with Britain condemning the slave trade. As Christopher Schmidt-Nowara has pointed out, Spanish liberalism opted for the expansion of slavery, while tightening control over the colonies. Between 1831 and 1840 some 181,600 African men, women, and children joined the enslaved labor force of the island.[67] The real drop took place in the 1840s when, first, the Spanish government, pressured by England, began to combat the illegal trade and, second, multiple slave rebellions convinced colonial officials of the need to "whiten" the island's population.[68] After 1845, fewer than three thousand slaves arrived per year, despite the continuing demand.[69]

The result was that, increasingly, masters and mistresses had to rely on the domestic market. As slaves became harder to find, their prices rose. Appraising a slave, when done properly, involved hiring an expert appraiser and a doctor, both of whom took into consideration, among other factors, the enslaved man's or woman's appearance, skills, age, health, disposition, and degree of assimilation to Creole society (the higher the degree, the better).[70] In the 1820s, a healthy enslaved man in his thirties who had a skill—for example, as a tailor—could typically be valued at 650 pesos, a thirty-year-old coachman at 600, or a twenty-two-year old pastry maker at 550, while a two-year-old enslaved child could be valued at 150 pesos, and a twenty-six-year-old washerwoman at 600 pesos. By 1860, the prices for all these categories had gone up considerably.

Despite the price of slaves, women from a wide range of social backgrounds owned slaves in nineteenth-century Cuba. For wealthy families, owning a small army of domestic slaves was a requirement—a way to make their lives comfortable and an indication of their social status; for women in the lower classes, buying and then hiring out slaves was a reliable source of income, a smart investment, and their best chance to achieve financial security.

At the time of her death in 1824, a Havana woman named Teresa O'Farrill, who came from an influential Creole family, owned hundreds of slaves on her sugar and coffee plantations, plus about twenty domestic servants in her Havana home who were appraised to be sold and distributed among her heirs. There were men, women, and children among the slaves for sale, all listed as "healthy and without flaws" in the inventory (which also specified their ethnic background). The male slaves included José Lorenzo Bustamante from Saint Domingue, about thirty-six years old, who was a tailor; a *mulato* named Ciriaco, about thirty years old, said to be a good coachman; a thirty-one-year-old named José Miguel who was a washerman; Domingo (Carabalí), about twenty-two, a pastry- and candy-maker; and Bonifacio (also Carabalí) twenty years old, listed as a good cook. The children included a *mulato* boy named Francisco, about two years old, and another one named Antonio, seven months old. The female slaves included a *mulata* named Ana María Guerrero (Creole), about twenty-six, who was a *dispensera* (pantry maid); Dolores (also Creole), about eighteen, a washerwoman and candy-maker; Sebastiana, identified as Mina, about seventeen, who had served as personal maid and seamstress; Agapita (Carabalí), about twenty, and a wet nurse; María (Mandinga), about twenty-six, a good washerwoman; and Rafaela (also Mandinga), about twenty-two years old, listed as a good cook.[71]

Middle-class women, as their wills reflect, had fewer slaves—usually between one and six, depending on their household needs, their economic power, and who performed the various arduous domestic activities required to run a nineteenth-century household: washing, cooking, cleaning, and making clothes, among other things. In the 1830s, Josefa Antonia González, a resident of Havana, had six grown slaves serving her large family: two men and four women, including two wet nurses.[72] By contrast, in 1852, Josefa Reyna, also from Havana, a homeowner with no children, had only one slave.[73]

Living in the poor parts of towns, often in crowded houses, both Black and white women of the lower classes still acquired slaves when possible—with the purpose of renting them out so that they would generate income.[74] Cuban historian Oilda Hevia Lanier has written a fascinating study of sixty women of African descent who were slave owners in Havana during the first six decades of the nineteenth century. Forty-five of them had themselves been brought as slaves from Africa; the rest came from different parts in the Caribbean or were natives of Havana. The author points out that for these women, trying to make it in a society where so much was stacked against them, owning slaves was "a survival strategy." Ownership of an enslaved person was an investment that allowed the women to gain social status, move up the economic ladder, and improve the quality of life for themselves and their families.[75] *Jornaleros* (hired-out slaves) tended to have more autonomy than other enslaved persons. They had to give their owners an arranged amount of money and could keep the rest for themselves, an ambiguous arrangement that led to multiple litigations. As fruit vendors, clothes sellers, cooks, wet nurses, carpenters, and tailors, they were an important part of urban public life. When visiting Santiago, which had a large French population, the British artist Walter Goodman mentioned the ubiquity of these workers: "Many of the less opulent Madamas of the town employ their time by making French pastry, which their slaves afterwards dispose of in the public streets. The Dulcera deals in 'dulces' and her cry of 'Dulce de guayaba! Dulce de almiba!' proclaims that her tray contains various kinds of West Indian preserves. The Dulcera is also a slave, and consequently derives no pecuniary benefit from the sale of her sweets, unless, by prearrangement with her owner, a share in the profits has been allowed."[76] The *dulce* seller in a sketch by Samuel Hazard is an example of the kind of *jornaleras* who filled the streets, squares, and markets of many Cuban towns (figure 1.3).

It is not surprising that money was a commonly contested issue and a continuous source of friction between mistresses who hired out slaves and those slaves themselves, the enslaved workers complaining that the amount they were required to turn over was excessive, and the slave owners arguing it was insufficient.[77] Closely connected to this conflict was another source of friction, a legal recourse a slave could use to achieve manumission, known as *coartación*.

The *coartación* was the most common strategy the enslaved population tried to rely on to achieve freedom. This legal arrangement could allow slaves to gradually buy their own freedom or that of their relatives. This tradition, sporadically present in medieval Spain, was accepted by every royal instruction that addressed the slaves' treatment, including the *Real Cédulas* of 1768, 1773, 1778, and 1789, and was codified into law by the 1842 *Reglamento de Esclavos*, and the *Reglamento para Síndicos in Havana* of 1863.[78] According to the colonial legal system, when a slaveholder and a slave agreed on a certain value and the slave provided the owner a percentage of that final amount, the slave could not be sold for a higher price and had to be freed once the total

Figure 1.3. *Dulce-Seller*, a rented-out slave, in Samuel Hazard, *Cuba with Pen and Pencil* (1871), 167.

amount had been paid. While never easy, this strategy had more chances to succeed in an urban setting, where there were opportunities for slaves, especially those with a skill, to save money little by little as hired workers. The result was a convoluted bureaucratic and legal reality by which slaves tried to prove that they were worth little so as to make it easier to purchase their own freedom, while slave owners tried to prove the opposite so as to increase their own financial position. As recent scholarship has demonstrated, it is fascinating to trace how astute the enslaved population was at finding cracks in the Spanish legal system.[79] According to Cuban historians Aisnara Perera and Maria de los Angeles Meriño, 71 percent of all litigations over *coartaciones* were brought against male slaveholders and 29 percent against female owners—not a surprising statistic, considering men had much greater economic power and had legal authority over their wives' affairs.[80] Rebecca

Scott has pointed out that as the price of slaves went up throughout the century, the possibility of *coartación* became more difficult for slaves to achieve, indeed, almost impossible. In 1871, she records 2,137 *esclavos coartados* (enslaved persons whose owner had agreed to set their price at a certain amount, which helped the enslaved buy their freedom, if they came up with the required amount), mostly in Havana, where the practice of hiring out was more common.[81]

When owners proved to be unreasonable or failed to keep their arrangement, slaves could seek help from the *síndico*, an official authority assigned to represent and protect slaves' interests in all sorts of matters, such as excessive punishment, poor treatment, or, in general, slaveholders' failure to fulfill their role as provider. Once again, asking for legal help was easier for town slaves than for those living on isolated plantations, where the owner's permission was required to leave and where the chances of meeting with someone who could explain how the system worked were far smaller. As was to be expected, masters and mistresses often challenged the *síndico*'s decisions, but the slaveholding class accepted the role of this official figure because he provided both a certain amount of order and the appearance of legitimacy to the institution of slavery.[82]

In 1854, a slave named Cecilia, feeling that her owner, doña Inés Hernández, mistreated her, tried to become *coartada* so that she could gradually buy her own freedom, and to that end gave her owner 100 pesos. Doña Inés had bought Cecilia for 600 pesos, and yet, only nine months later, when the slave asked to be *coartada*, the mistress raised her price to 800, making it prohibitive for the enslaved woman to acquire enough money to achieve her goal. Cecilia then filed a complaint with the *síndico*, who recorded the following:

> The *morena* Cecilia Creole to Your Excellency with due respect states that her mistress doña Inés Hernández has not fulfilled her duty with the supplicant not even with a minimum of her expected humane obligations. Since she has been in her power, for the last nine months, she hasn't even received a handkerchief: when she was sick, she made her get up from bed to work to the point that she fainted; having given birth at home, the exponent herself had to pay the midwife and even the food from her small savings she had collected from her previous owners' gifts. Unable to suffer such inhumane treatment, she tried to *coartarse* with a payment of 100 pesos to that end, and the mistress, who had only paid for the exponent 600 pesos . . . today demands 800 pesos and the rights, an excessive amount no one wants to give for a servant in poor health and who cannot perform any task with great skill since to this date her main occupation has been to be a wet nurse.

What followed was an arduous negotiation, mediated by the *síndico*, between the enslaved woman and her owner, which finally came to a resolution both sides agreed on: "after a long conference," the *síndico* wrote, Cecilia was *coartada* (with her price set at 628 pesos), and her mistress gave her the papers to look for a new owner.[83]

In some cases, and when trying to make up the difference between their wages and what a mistress demanded, slaves could even be forced into prostitution or stealing.[84] Slaveholders had forced women slaves to work as prostitutes since the early 1600s, a practice that continued through the mid-1800s, especially in port cities like Havana and Santiago with large itinerant male populations that included sailors, soldiers, and immigrants.[85] Already in the mid-1700s, the government's guidelines asked slaveholders to refrain from demanding excessive payments from the slaves they rented out in order to avoid immorality, and requested that they should not be too harsh, in order to prevent "harm to the souls of these people,"[86] the latter a futile request that was hard to enforce.

In December 1866 in Havana, a slave named Salomé Giménez filed a complaint with her *síndico* denouncing her mistress, Sebastiana Puig, for demanding 19 pesos and 4 reales (silver coins) per month of her wages, an expectation she could not meet. The enslaved woman had been valued at 1,250 pesos, and she had already paid 650 pesos for her *coartación*, leaving 600 pesos that she needed to raise with her work in order to get her manumission status. The *síndico* sent Salomé to one of the municipal *depósitos* where slaves in conflict with their masters could live temporarily while a judge made a ruling, and then conferred with doña Sebastiana.[87] The mistress argued that she had purchased the enslaved woman with the condition to receive monthly wages; she complained that the slave had failed to comply for months, had expressed her desire to find a new mistress, and had refused to return to her owner's home. What ensued was a long back-and-forth between all participants with the slaveholder ignoring many of the citations with the excuse that she was gravely ill, and filing a complaint against the slave representative for being unfair. On his note to the judge, the *síndico*, citing the 1864 *Reglamento de Síndicos*, sided with Salomé Giménez and pointed out the impossibility for a slave woman to make so much money unless, he implied, she prostituted herself: "Your excellency will understand," wrote the *síndico*, "that a slave woman can make a maximum of 17 or 20 pesos per month, considering the need to discount Sundays and other holidays; in order to meet the demand the slave would have to make 40 pesos per month, which is repugnant to our customs, to our morality, and could not be authorized." The judge, agreeing with the *síndico*, ruled that the slave should remain in the municipal *depósito* and that the matter of wages should be resolved according to the law as stated in the *Reglamento*.[88]

The absurdity of the slave system became more obvious in the case of *jornaleros,* who fully supported themselves with their wages, and particularly when the owners failed to fulfill their obligations as slaveholders. In May 1866, José Herrera, a Havana *jornalero*, asked for his freedom based on the complaint that his owner, doña Mercedes Casanova, did not provide him with clothes and shoes. The *síndico*, Antonio Bachiller Morales, who would become a renowned historian, moved the slave to a *depósito* while negotiations for his freedom took place. An angry mistress challenged the *síndico*'s decision, removed the slave from the *depósito,* and brought him home. The final resolution of this case is unknown.[89]

If there was no conflict and a slave managed to meet the price of the stipulated *coartación*, a legal document was issued to formalize that the slaveholder no longer held power over the enslaved man or woman. Following a common format, the 1846 letter of manumission for Prudenciana, a resident of Santiago de Cuba, stated that she had paid 450 pesos in exchange for her freedom. Having received the said amount, her mistress, María Josefa de Hechavarría, granted full freedom to her former slave; renounced any patronage, property, or other rights she had previously enjoyed; and transferred to Prudenciana the power to hire, go to trial, and do all other acts free people were capable of, so that she would never be subjected to servitude again.[90]

The same year and also in Santiago de Cuba, an enslaved woman, movingly, managed to pay not for her own freedom, but for that of her two-year-old son, as the letter of manumission signed by the child's mistress indicated: "Be it known that I, Carmen Caballero . . . owner of Juan Bautista, creole, two years of age . . . have received from his mother, *la negra* Francisca de Borja, doña Margarita Caballero's slave, 100 pesos for his freedom, which I acknowledge to have received in common currency and estimate to be currently his fair value . . . granting the said Juan Bautista full freedom."[91] As an urban slave, Francisca de Borja must have painstakingly saved enough money to buy freedom for her son, if not for herself. Who knows how many hours she had to work to come up with the 100 pesos she paid her son's mistress. That feat was even harder to achieve for a plantation slave, who had fewer chances to earn money, as we will see in the following chapter.

CONCLUSION

Cuba's nineteenth-century economic boom resulted in the enormous expansion of the enslaved population, many of whom were destined to work as domestic slaves or as hired-out workers in the island's urban centers. The institution of slavery turned the home into an extension of the slave market.

The availability of slaves was so great that owning them became common not only among the wealthy but also among the middle and even the lower classes. The institution of slavery shaped the lives and values of the master class. Poorly educated and with few opportunities for self-expression, slaveholding women were often defenders of the status quo, despite the growing acceptance of modern values on the part of the middle class. Slavery allowed white women to run efficient households. Enslaved servants cleaned, cooked, repaired, washed, and took care of the white family's needs, while also providing the owners with a symbol of social success. As head of the private sphere, mistresses had a significant role in controlling the purchase and work of their domestic labor force. The print media's frequent ads reveal what they were looking for when they acquired an enslaved man, woman, or child. Inevitably, tension was common between slaveholders and the people whose lives they controlled, tension that could lead to slaves' attempts to purchase their own freedom (*coartarse*), to ask for the *síndico*'s help, or to run away.

2

Visiting the Sugar Mill

EACH YEAR, AS the Christmas holidays neared, the Cuban slaveholding class got ready to leave their town homes and to spend time in the country. Cuban plantation mistresses visited their sugar mills (*ingenios*) once or twice a year, often in December, at the beginning of the harvest season, and in the spring, coinciding with Easter. These visits gave the white women a chance to play a role in the functioning of the plantations, and to have an impact on the lives of the enslaved men, women, and children who toiled for them and their families. Though seemingly inconsequential, those temporary stays, whether happy or tense occasions, in fact helped cement a power structure and culture that condoned slavery.

There had been sugar mills in Cuba since the late 1500s, but they tended to be small, modest operations. It was not until the nineteenth century, when large numbers of enslaved men, women, and children were available, that the sugar plantation economy thrived, with the western and central parts of the island becoming home to enormously profitable *ingenios*. Mistresses of plantations were members of a privileged class; their wealth, through inheritance or marriage, was based on the work of enslaved plantation workers. In most cases these women were *criolla* (Creole)—that is, born in Cuba and of Spanish descent—but some were French, American, German, or *peninsulares*. As members of the elite, they were highly influential, their behavior and ideas helping shape the dominant culture.

An anonymous engraving, inspired by the work of French artist Frédéric Mialhe and included in *Album pintoresco de la isla de Cuba,* edited by Bernard May in 1853, depicts the boiling house of a typical Cuban sugar plantation. The image portrays several slaves busy at work, boiling and refining sugar, while supervised by a white man. In the middle of the room, two white men, likely the plantation owner and one of his employees, talk business. In

Figure 2.1. *View of a Boiling House in Cuba (Vista de una casa de calderas de la isla de Cuba),* artist unknown. In *Album pintoresco de la isla de Cuba*, ed. Bernardo May (1853), engraving 26. BNJM, Libros Raros y Valiosos.

one corner, an unusual scene unfolds: two white women sitting on chairs are being served a drink by a slave (figure 2.1).[1]

Did white women really spend time inside the hot boiling room where sugar was produced? This is the type of question that plantation logs, census records, and government documents fail to clarify, but that more subjective documents, such as memoirs and fiction, may address. Once again, in Cirilo Villaverde's *Cecilia Valdes*, which captured Creole society so accurately, we find a possible answer to the surprising scene. In this novel, the slaveholding Gamboa family travels from Havana to their plantation with a group of guests for the Christmas holiday, as was common practice in nineteenth-century Cuba. Slaveholders often encouraged their friends to visit their country homes, and they opened them to travelers, their legendary hospitality both a tradition and a way to relieve the boredom of living removed from society.

The slave owners and their friends did not have many amusements to entertain them on their properties, which tended to be in rural, isolated spots. One of the distractions they did have during their stay was to visit the various facilities where sugar was produced, including the boiling house, and that is precisely what the Gamboas decide to do one evening in the company of their guests. When the masters arrive, the slaves continue to perform their exhausting tasks, which during harvest season could last up to fourteen hours a day. Chairs are brought to a corner of the big room, where the slaveholders are seated and made comfortable. While the sugar master, one of those hired experts in sugar extraction techniques who were employed on all large plantations, proceeds to explain the process of making sugar and the machinery used for this purpose, the house slaves serve the plantation owners and their friends *guarapo* (a sugary drink to which a few drops of brandy have been added), a soothing beverage they welcome on this cool winter evening. But the illusion of being in a hospitable, pleasant environment is shattered irrevocably when they are all startled by the sound of a slave being whipped, making it difficult to continue with the social pleasantries as if nothing had happened: "The sudden crack of the whip on the opposite side of the boiler house just as Isabel"—one of the young guests—"was raising the beverage to her lips made her shudder from head to foot, and in her confusion the cup slipped from her hands."[2] The scene resonates on many levels: it captures the slave owners' failed attempt to pretend that plantations were a hospitable environment, a suitable destination for a pleasant vacation for both slaveholders and their guests. It also places white women at the heart of that delusion. The women's role is to play along with that mockery, to be silent and complicit during those brief stays.

"A sugar mill, especially a large sugar mill," wrote Antonio Zambrana in his abolitionist novel *El Negro Francisco* (1873), "is like a separate small kingdom in the middle of the country, something similar to the feudal states in the Middle Ages."[3] Including features of both an efficient factory and an isolated plantation, as a sketch by Samuel Hazard reflects, an *ingenio* was not a welcoming environment (figure 2.2). Absenteeism was a common feature among Cuban slaveholders, who spent as little time as possible on their sugar plantations. Coffee plantations, as we will see, were a different story. Only the owners of small sugar plantations, who could not afford to keep two residences, lived on their estates.[4] For that reason, a visit from the master and mistress was a momentous occasion. In his novel Zambrana characterized the slaveholders' arrival at their plantation, Esperanza, as an exciting time for the slaves, who came out to greet the family: "They arrived at the Plantation and the servants came happily to greet them."[5] In February 1828, in a letter to her family in Massachusetts, Margaret Quincy, a guest at a plantation, also described the scene of the master and mistress's arrival at their property as a happy one: "As we rode along, the negroes ran to meet the carriages [*volantes*] seeming delighted at again seeing their master and mistress."[6]

But for all the initial excitement, the contact between the two groups (the visitors and the enslaved men and women), tended to be guarded and fraught with tension. In his series of articles on slavery published as a collection in

Figure 2.2. *Ingenio Carolina*, in Samuel Hazard, *Cuba with Pen and Pencil* (1871), 402.

1859, the writer Anselmo Suárez y Romero left testimony of the intense interaction that could take place during those brief encounters. For the slaves, and especially for the field slaves, meeting the plantation owners was at best a chance to voice their concerns, an opportunity to improve their living conditions: "As soon as they dropped the grass on the heap, the oldest and wisest among them walked to the big house, while the others stayed waiting for him, all grouped together a short distance away. He came to ask for permission to dance and drum as a way to celebrate the masters' arrival. Soon after, the old man returned with the others, their shouting and running clearly indicating that his request had been granted."[7] In the midst of the brutal living conditions that they were forced to endure, historian Salvador Morales Pérez reminds us, Cuban slaves carried within themselves an individual agency that planned for the future and came up with strategies to improve it. He writes, "That planning implied more than a mere desire to be free, it implied knowledge, interest in the means that would help move forward in the desired direction."[8]

During the masters' visits, one of the strategies to better their lives was to let their owners know their opinions, and one of the few means field slaves could use to do this was through their singing. In "La Casa del Trapiche" (1853), Suárez y Romero explains how the songs the enslaved men and women sang while working chronicled all the important events happening on the plantation: the death of an animal, a fire, a runaway being caught, or the arrival of the slaveholders. And when slaves knew the owners were listening, the improvised lyrics referred to the plantation owners themselves, whether as a way to thank the master and mistress (for a new set of clothes that slaves had received, for permission for several couples to marry the next Sunday, for removal of a slave's shackles) or, on the contrary, as a way to complain about how slaves were treated (made to work longer hours or not given enough food).[9]

In "El Corte de Caña" (1859), another article in the same collection, Suárez y Romero describes a visit by a group of friends to his family plantation, which, like that of the Gamboa family in *Cecilia Valdés*, included being entertained by slaves' daily activities. The plantation owner and his guests dance, drink champagne, and eat delicacies served on exquisite china. They then consider various options for an outdoors activity: should they explore the forest or walk by the canal, visit the river or admire the garden? But when they hear the carts heavy with sugar cane approach, the group of young people decide to go find amusement in watching slaves work, a scene they agree can be described as a magnificent canvas. During this encounter, slaves and masters observe each other—especially, Suárez y Romero tells us, the women on both sides. As the slaves continue to labor and sweat, an old man breaks into a song with lyrics directed to his observers. The slaves are well treated and given enough food, the old man explains, but they are so tired they have a hard time keeping awake. When the song finishes, the slaves ask for the white people's blessing, and are grateful to receive that and a few coins from them—all, that is, except for a slave who is wearing shackles as punishment for his rebellious nature, and who stays apart. One of the *señoritas* intercedes for him, a role that women were expected to play, and the chains are removed. At the end of the evening, the female guests are offered a bouquet of flowers to take with them, and they leave happily after what they think was a delightful visit. The writer lets the reader know he has been left with an uneasy feeling, but he fails to tell us whether he reconsidered the number of hours his slaves were asked to work.[10]

Suárez y Romero's ambiguity is not surprising: he belonged to that conflicted Cuban intellectual class who wrote about and proclaimed the evils of slavery, while owning slaves and living off the profits of their plantations. This group was led by Domingo del Monte, a literary patron, and a key figure in helping Juan Francisco Manzano (discussed in chapter 1) achieve his freedom. They thought of themselves as modern men and chastised the institution of slavery, which they viewed as a deterrent to modernization, yet their families had invested large sums of money buying slaves, and they were not courageous enough to advocate abolition, other than in a vague, distant future. Del Monte, for example, and as Christopher Schmidt-Nowara has pointed out, was himself "connected by marriage and patronage to two of the most prominent slaveholding families in Cuba: the powerful Aldama and Alfonso families, important creole planters." As such, "he firmly defended the interests of slaveowners and feared Cuban slaves and free people of color in general."[11] When they wrote fiction, their depictions—as in the case of Suárez y Romero, but also in the case of Cirilo Villaverde, Antonio Zambrana, and many other antislavery writers—failed to reflect the reality of the African-descended Cubans, who were often portrayed in the worst stereotypical, Romantic manner that was fashionable at the time. Cuban historian Manuel Moreno Fraginals writes that Suárez y Romero recorded details of the traumatic lives of slaves without being able to interpret them, "like the narration of a dumb child describing a crime without understanding it."[12] But for all his failings in the portrayal of the slaves' reality, Suárez y Romero's descriptions of the slaveholding class were accurate and realistic. He knew his people well, as his articles on slavery demonstrate.

If the owners' visits to the plantation offered slaves a chance to voice their concerns, for the masters and mistresses, a temporary stay on their properties provided opportunities to display control and solidify their status as rulers. The occasion served as a reminder of slaveholders' power to punish and forgive, with their harshness or magnanimity helping strengthen their position as godlike figures whose decisions could forever alter slaves' destiny. In *Cecilia Valdés*, during the master and mistress's visit, as was typical on those occasions, twenty-seven newly bought slaves were baptized and several slaves were married, "whose wishes in the matter"—denounces the writer—"were not examined, not even for form's sake."[13] In "Domingos en los ingenios" (1840), yet another of Suárez y Romero's articles on slavery, the writer refers to the female slaves who brought their children to the masters after being baptized: "I hear the chattering of many black women leaving their huts and approaching the house. It's probably a baptism, and before going to the village, they will come to be seen by the masters."[14]

The temporary nature of the planters' stay on their *ingenios* was particularly significant for women, their rare visits being filled with potential, if not always actual, consequences. While their visits lasted, mistresses' presence at the sugar mill served as an opportunity to reward or punish slaves, a chance to mediate conflicts and make decisions that would have lasting impact on the lives of the enslaved men and women. It was during those stays, for instance, that mistresses selected from among the children those who would become the house slaves: as Suárez y Romero put it, "the occasion when the mistress picks among the young slaves the one she'll take to live in the big house."[15] In his autobiography (discussed in chapter 1), Juan Francisco Manzano recalled how his mistress liked to pick her house slaves during those visits: "Whenever doña Beatriz de Justiz, the Marchioness Justiz de Santa Ana, . . . went to El Molino, her famous plantation, she liked to take with her the most beautiful ten- and eleven-year-old Creole girls. She took them along, providing them with appropriate upbringing for their class and station in society."[16]

Those brief visits also served the purpose of maintaining—though in some cases they shattered—the illusion of a mistress as a benevolent figure, and the plantation as a humane environment where slaves' physical and spiritual needs were addressed.

In "Su Retrato" ("Her Portrait," 1855), Suárez y Romero defined the characteristics of a good Cuban woman and mistress. Her virtues included a thorough knowledge of and love for the island, a fondness for reading, a familiarity with geography and history, and, when married, being a good slaveholder, whose advice was listened to by her children and her slaves, all of whom benefited from her moral influence over them. "Compassion and fairness, harmony and contentment, calmness and orderliness will preside over her world. Wrath will never disturb her sweet face's expression. Children and slaves will listen to her reprimands and advice," Suárez y Romero wrote.[17]

One of the crucial roles mistresses were expected to play was that of helping soften the harsh conditions of the enslaved population. In nineteenth-century Cuba, not unlike in the United States and Europe, the female ideal emphasized women's purity, virtue, and compassion, qualities that placed women in a perfect position to act as kind mediators and a mission the Catholic world could easily connect to the Virgin Mary and her role to intercede with God in favor of sinners.[18] Religion shaped the lives of Cuban women: observing the Catholic calendar, attending mass, and celebrating baptisms, first communions, and weddings punctuated women's existence. Moreover, through public sermons delivered from the pulpit, and in their capacity as personal confessors, church officials helped define the nineteenth-century female ideal both in Spain and in Cuba. Figures like Antonio María Claret, a prolific and influential writer of sermons, who served as archbishop of Santiago de Cuba in the 1850s, encouraged their female parishioners to identify with and to follow the example of the Virgin Mary. Women should be pious, quiet, and patient; they should obey their husbands; they should be humble, chaste, and devoted to their families.[19] It was also their duty to be merciful. By behaving in a compassionate manner, women, as protective figures, were expected to ease the most inhumane aspects of the institution of slavery. "The good mistress" (*el ama buena*) was devoted to her slaves and adored by them. She objected to the use of the whip to punish slaves who had misbehaved, she visited sick slaves in the infirmary, and she played her nurturing role in a motherly, loving fashion, leaving her slaves devastated when she left the plantation. Mercedes Santa Cruz y Montalvo, the countess of Merlín, a Cuban aristocrat, perpetuated the image of the good, motherly mistress when she characterized her aunt Antonia, the family's matriarch, as a saint. Like Domingo del Monte and other members of the Creole elite, Merlín was critical of the slave trade and of Spain's management of Cuba, yet a firm proponent of maintaining the institution of slavery and a believer in slaveholders' beneficent role.[20] Ignoring the fact that it was slaves' work that allowed slaveholders to maintain their lavish standard of living, she wrote: "My aunt Antonia is a saint, she herself makes the layettes for her negro women and sends part of the best food from her table to her old or sick slaves. She never scolds her negroes, on the contrary she allows them all kind of laziness and mistakes, so much so that, except at lunch time, you'll find her negro women lying on the ground all day on bamboo rugs, singing, chatting and combing each other's hair."[21]

Isabel Illincheta, the aforementioned character in *Cecilia Valdés*, and Carlota, in Gertrudis Gómez de Avellaneda's *Sab*, are female figures in nineteenth-century Cuban fiction who embody the "good mistress." Isabel is a young slaveholder who performs her duties admirably: she visits the sick slaves in the infirmary, takes their pulse, and suggests ways to relieve their fever; she instructs the overseer not to use the whip as punishment, and as a result is viewed as a true angel by her slaves, who consider her "the most beautiful and kindliest of women, a delicate and supernatural being."[22] "Po' slave cry," they lament before Isabel's departure from the plantation.[23] Carlota, the young slaveholder in *Sab* is also a good example of the humane mistress, and her concern for slaves' welfare is rewarded with their love and loyalty. "Carlota was interrupted in her innocent amusements by the bustle of the slaves going off to work. She called to them, asking their names one by one, and enquiring with enchanted kindness about each one's particular situation, position, and state of being . . . Carlota enjoyed listening to them and, with words of compassion and affection, divided among them what money she had in her pockets. The slaves went off still blessing her, and she looked at them with brimming eyes."[24]

But just as often, Cuban literature has provided examples of mistresses who failed to conform to the ideal of the Christian and compassionate female slaveholder. The bad mistress is a recurrent character in Cuban literature, where she tends to be more prominent than her husband, who is hardly mentioned in many works of fiction. The critique is not so much of her role as a slaveholder, as of the fact that she fails to perform her role well, her deficiencies undermining paternalistic notions that would have eased plantation life.

Anselmo Suárez y Romero's *Francisco, el ingenio o las delicias del campo* was written in 1839, making it one of the earliest antislavery novels—though it was not published until 1880. In this work, the mistress, doña Dolores Mendizábal, a wealthy lady from Havana, avoids the plantation as much as possible, and when she finally visits during the Christmas holidays, she spends most of her time in her own living quarters. In a weak attempt to fulfill her role, she pays a visit to the infirmary, but leaves right away because of the bad smell.[25] Critics like Suárez were angered by female slaveholders who failed to live up to the "good mistress" ideal, and denounced their hypocrisy. Doña Dolores justifies her reluctance to confront the slaves' living conditions as a sign of her delicacy, an indication of her kind heart. The mistress in *Francisco* avoids the area where slaves are physically punished with the stock because, she claims, she feels sorry for those who are subjected to it—and yet she is the one responsible for the punishment.[26]

More often than not, female slaveholders' avoidance of the *ingenio* had to do with the lack of social amenities or comforts found on a typical plantation, in comparison to a town house, but that unwillingness could also have a more personal dimension. The plantation was viewed as the natural destination for the house slave who had misbehaved. As the British consul and famed abolitionist David Turnbull wrote: "The worst threat wealthy Havana men and women could make to terrorize their house slaves if they misbehaved was to send them to the country."[27] Cuban literature is filled with examples of slaves who, having offended their mistresses, are sent to the plantation as punishment for what the ladies deem immoral behavior (often a manifestation of sexual rivalry) and as a way to get them out of the masters' way. Slavery created insecurity and anxiety in white women's married life. We have scant direct information about this because of how taboo the subject was and how few personal accounts Cuban women left, but sexual interaction between masters and enslaved women is one of nineteenth-century Cuban fiction's recurring themes. That and demographic evidence of racial mingling suggests that husbands' unfaithfulness was a common preoccupation in the *señoras'* family life.

In Félix Tanco Bosmeniel's *Petrona y Rosalía* (1838), when the mistress realizes her slave Petrona is pregnant, her moral outrage makes her send the young woman to the plantation to cut cane, be whipped, and have her hair shorn. When the master mildly intercedes to recommend a more benign punishment, his wife responds indignantly that she cannot allow such indecent behavior in her home, as it would set a bad example for their son. Petrona bears a light-skinned girl, who is in fact the master's daughter. The girl, repeating the cycle, grows up to be raped by the master's son, her half-brother. In turn, she is sent to work at the plantations and dies in childbirth.[28]

The assumption that a mistress was the one in charge of enforcing her family's moral standards and obedience to church doctrine could be used to rationalize a punitive action against slaves when they were accused of failing to uphold those godly values, or simply as a way to sanction her detachment from the cruelty of slavery. In Antonio Zambrana's *El Negro Francisco*, the plantation owner, doña Josefa, rarely sees her slaves: "In the country she was devoted to praying. She was almost always in the chapel."[29] Religion also helped justify the institution of slavery itself in the eyes of slaveholding women, given the pull the Catholic Church had in shaping her views. The argument, repeated often from the pulpit, that she played a crucial role in saving her slaves' souls from damnation by instilling Christian values was a reassuring idea. Nineteenth-century Cuban and Spanish liberals viewed the church as a remnant of the old régime, an obstacle to modernization. They denounced the clergy's defense of the social order as divinely ordained, an apt critique when it came to the enslaved. Despite some notable exceptions (including Father Félix Varela, an influential Cuban political figure in favor of abolition, or the aforementioned Archbishop Claret, who antagonized the slaveholding class with his attacks on their treatment of the enslaved), most religious authorities sanctioned the institution of slavery. Many priests and nuns owned slaves themselves.[30] But the role of religion was complex. Some slaveholding women took seriously their obligation to render slavery more humane in accordance with Christian ideals. The two institutions, slavery and the Catholic Church, worked in a tenuous balance to create the conflicted moral framework the white Cuban woman lived by. The contradictions between the two sets of values were often highlighted in nineteenth-century fiction. Doña Rosa, the slave owner in *Cecilia Valdés*, is described as "a Christian woman who was kind to her equals, who frequently made confessions, who gave alms to the poor, who adored her children."[31] Yet she remains unmoved when she sees her slaves contorted by pain under the whip. She, like many women in her situation, has become desensitized by her long exposure to the slave system.

Do nineteenth-century Cuban novels, many of them with an abolitionist bent, exaggerate the repressive regime that slaves lived under? Did the religious values of the slaveholding class influence its behavior? Tension between paternalism and productivity, between the Christian ideal of treating slaves with compassion and the desire to increase profits had been evident since the beginning of the sugar boom in the late eighteenth century. Before the Cuban plantation economy became enormously profitable, both government authorities and slave owners took somewhat seriously the importance of converting the African population to Christianity. Alejandro de la Fuente records that, in the 1500s and 1600s, slaves were expected to pray and learn the Christian precepts after supper every night.[32] Instructions for overseers that circulated in Havana in the 1780s stated with naive determination the importance of guaranteeing slaves, including *bozales* (recent arrivals), enough free time for religious instruction. *Negros* (a term used indistinctly in nineteenth-century Cuba to refer to Black people and the enslaved) who were not Christians were to be sent every night to the chaplain or overseer to be taught the Commandments until they were ready to be baptized. The overseer, the document explained, should not be content with reading the instructions once, but should do it multiple times until the information had been understood.[33]

As late as 1789, and illustrating the wide chasm between the official rhetoric and the reality that plantation slaves endured, the crown issued a royal decree reminding Cuban slaveholders of their obligation to instruct their slaves in the tenets of the Catholic religion, even if that interfered with their work schedule, and exhorting the planter class to make sure that slaves prayed the rosary every night after work with the "greatest composure and devotion."[34] The decree also ordered that enslaved people be provided with comfortable quarters when they were sick, be allowed to marry whom they chose, not be punished with excessive force, and many other measures aimed at alleviating the conditions that slaves lived under.[35] As Ada Ferrer has pointed out, seventy-one plantation owners, including twelve women, immediately signed a petition contesting the crown's regulations.[36] They argued that the implementation of those rules would have a dismal effect on productivity and would result in the ruin of their families and the royal treasury. In short, the rules simply could not be carried out.[37] The government was easily convinced, leaving the church alone with its faint attempts to resist the expanding influence of the world market.

In 1796, Antonio Nicolás Duque de Estrada, a priest from Havana, published a catechism that aimed to teach enslaved people the Catholic doctrine, including obscure concepts such as the Holy Trinity.[38] Initiatives such as this one were nonsensical. More substantial efforts to improve slaves' plights, argued Robert L. Paquette in his classic *Sugar Is Made with Blood*, were defeated. "The Church fought and lost the struggle for orthodoxy in the countryside at the turn of the century when the Crown agreed with the planters' demand to liberate the plantation from religious burdens such as meatless Fridays, work-free Sundays and holidays, and the all-important tithe."[39] Slaveholders put any humanitarian concern aside to achieve maximum profits. In 1842, the colonial government's new attempt to improve the lives of slaves and stimulate their reproduction resulted in the Slave Code, a new set of guidelines for plantation owners. Many of the code's rules included provisions that could be construed as falling into a mistress's realm, and therefore under her purview. The code adjured slave owners to instruct their slaves in the principles of the Catholic religion. Religious instruction should be conducted in the evening upon the conclusion of the workday, and should be followed by praying the rosary. On Sundays, slaves could be asked to do domestic chores only for up to two hours, unless work demands were pressing. Owners were encouraged to teach their slaves the need to obey the authorities, respect white people, and live in good harmony with their fellow slaves. Other guidelines referred to the proper amount of food the field hands required, the clothing that slaveholders should provide, and the care of infants, as well as of the sick.[40] In other words, mistresses who took these guidelines seriously could potentially ameliorate some of the harsher aspects of slaves' living conditions. But by the 1840s, at the height of the sugar boom, and after several slave rebellions had shaken the sugar elite to the core, few slaveholders bothered to comply with the guidelines. Indeed, slaveholders, encouraged by the enormous profits produced by the sugar industry and fearful that Cuba could suffer Saint Domingue's fate and experience a slave revolution, increased disciplinary measures against the enslaved people under their control. Their anxiety was exacerbated by the fact that in the 1840s, slaves and free people of color together outnumbered the white population.

Some historians have argued that harsh treatment of the enslaved population was bad for business, and that, to some degree, the best run *ingenios* and *cafetales* were those where ill-treatment was kept to a minimum. Cuban historian Gloria García pointed out that the successful operation of a plantation involved a combination of force and flexibility on the part of the planter, a satisfactory interrelation between the human components that carried out those activities. "The daily routine on both the *ingenio* and *cafetal* depended on such a delicate equilibrium and not simply on blind obedience to the owner."[41] It is likely that, when possible, slaveholders preferred the role of benefactor over that of firm disciplinarian, as their benevolence helped maintain the illusion, even to themselves, of the plantation as a caring environment, their amiability contributing to the smooth functioning of the plantation's operations. For women of the planter class, their temporary visits were their chance to display their compassion and generosity.

Many travelers described how the masters and mistresses during the Christmas season (as mentioned, a typical time for plantation owners to visit their property) used their stays to play the role of magnanimous masters and to forgive those slaves who had broken the rules. Margaret Quincy wrote to her family that at Reserva, a plantation in Matanzas owned by an American couple where she spent some time, offenders were pardoned on New Year's Day, and all the men and women received "a quarter of a dollar, and a suit of new clothes."[42] Abiel Abbot, an American minister who traveled to Cuba for health reasons, described a similar scene when visiting the sugar mill La

Recompensa in 1828: "[New Year's Day] is the negro's red-letter day on this estate. On this day no work whatever is done; it is entirely given up to mirth and festivity. All liberties, except crimes, are permitted. At three in the morning, they make a general rush upon their master, and wish him a happy new year. Each receives a handkerchief as a present. Pardons are distributed in all cases, except of crimes which the laws of the land proscribe."[43] He approvingly explained how the slaves had been taught to ask their masters' blessing: "You cannot pass a half dozen little Creoles, without hearing their cheerful voices commending you to God; and the same thing happens in passing men and women in the field . . . These customs on the part of slaves, which wear an affectionate and religious aspect towards their superiors, it is the soundest policy in masters to encourage, while at the same time it somewhat lightens the yoke of bondage on their necks. They have the pleasure to see, that they are recognized as the humble children of their master."[44]

But while slaveholders tried to show their plantations in a positive light, maintaining the image of their property as a happy environment was not easy. Like the whipping at the boiling house portrayed in *Cecilia Valdes*, discussed at the beginning of this chapter, reality spoiled the picturesque scene that Abiel Abbot expected to see when he was invited to attend the inauguration of a new sugar plantation. As the guests arrived, all was joy and activity, Abbot wrote. The slaves cheered, and whipped and goaded the oxen; some brought the cane; others fed the nuts (the mechanical sections of the mill that grind and crush the cane); one or two stood at the back side to return the cane through the second pair of nuts, still others received the cane as it fell and distributed it in the path of the oxen, or carried it out in baskets to dry for fuel. The kettle was soon filled, the fire kindled, the process of making sugar begun. "In the midst of this busy, tumultuous, and noisy scene, a loud shriek at the mill, and a sudden stop of the oxen, and an instant's dead silence, and a countenance announce an accident . . . The hand of the man who was feeding the return nuts was caught, and his fingers and thumb drawn in nearly to the joint of the palm before the team could be arrested."[45] The former excitement, Abbot reported, turned into sadness.

Like Abbot, travelers and friends, as well as masters and mistresses on visits to their property, could not avoid seeing the signs of the slaves' unhappiness: the security measures surrounding their living quarters to prevent their escape, the harsh punishments meted out to those who violated the rules, the runaway slaves, the suicides. Ada Ferrer has written extensively on how the Cuban planter class learned a lesson from Haiti's revolution, the next-door neighbor serving as a dire warning of what could happen if discipline was relaxed.[46] Often visitors intertwined references to the horrors they saw with comments about the beauty of the plantations, the pleasant rides on horseback and in *volantes*, the shady woods and fresh creeks, the colorful birds, and the sumptuous meals enjoyed during their stay. Their conflicted descriptions accurately reflect the two widely different worlds slaves and planters inhabited. Margaret Quincy described in a letter to her family her visit to a sugar mill: "Our time passed swiftly in reading, working on the piazzas, playing with the children, listening to the Harp or Piano, and riding on horseback early in the morning, and it is delightful I assure you . . . I can give you no idea of these plantations by description."[47] Yet when her slaveholding friends threw a few coins to the begging slaves who surrounded them on one occasion, she found the chaos that ensued disturbing: "The confusion that followed frightened me, and the sight of so many human beings in so degraded a condition was so painful to me, that I went to my room, where I remained till I thought they must be dispersed."[48]

Frederika Bremer, a Swedish traveler who spent several months in Cuba in 1851 and left a written chronicle about her experience, also shows the ambivalence many foreign visitors felt about this institution. From her descriptions, we get glimpses, quick portraits of the island mistresses from various geographic backgrounds (mostly English- and French-speaking because she spoke their languages and could communicate with them). Bremer often expressed her distaste for slavery. She was fully aware of the conditions the enslaved lived under: their dark, unventilated, and dirty bedrooms; the infirmary without pillows, blankets, or real doctors to attend the sick (all this in contrast with the owners' comfortable domestic environment). Yet she was willing to believe that when slaveholders were kind, the system worked. She had nothing but praise for the many slaveholding women she befriended throughout her trip. "That kind, cordially good Mrs. F."—she wrote about her hostess in Havana—"was up with me at five o'clock the next morning, and had coffee brought for me and herself from a Restaurateur's, because she would not disturb her slaves so early."[49] Bremer visited the Yumurí Valley, which she described as a paradise, with its beautiful palm trees and mirror-like river, its green shrubs and mangrove trees. Mrs. Baley, her hostess, a young and beautiful slaveholding woman, provided her with Cecilia, a slave companion who spoke English, to serve as interpreter; Cecilia had been taken from the African coast when she was eight years old. The mistress wanted Cecilia, who was dying of consumption, to enjoy the fresh air of the country. After finding out how homesick Cecilia was for Africa and how much she missed her mother, Bremer made herself feel better by thinking that the slave would soon see her mother in heaven.[50]

In April 1851, Bremer arrived at the *ingenio* Santa Amelia, a very large plantation, and described the American mistress, Mrs. Coninck, as charming, agreeable, and well bred. As a widow, the plantation owner had full control of her property and was able to make her own decisions in regard to the treatment that slaves received. On her plantation, slaves worked with much severity: "They were allowed only four and a half hours out of the four-and-twenty for rest; that is to say for their meals and sleep, and that during six or seven months a year!"[51] But Bremer was reassured by the idea that slaves were used to that work schedule. Yet, while commenting on the splendid architecture of the plantations, and the beauty of the Cuban atmosphere, she could not avoid seeing multiple examples of the devastating impact of slavery: "It is not long since eleven Luccomees [an ethnic group] were found hanging from the branches of a guasima tree," she wrote in a letter recounting a mass suicide.[52]

Despite the many disturbing scenes she encountered, Bremer maintained her faith in the power of a good-natured mistress to assuage the cruelty of the institution. As her tour of the island continued, she recorded examples of *amas buenas* who had a beneficial influence on their slaves' lives. Bremer recounted the story of a Mr. Chapeaud, a French planter in Cuba who had to go abroad for a few months, leaving his property in the hands of an overseer, who proved so ruthless that he nearly caused a slave rebellion. After firing the man, Madame Chapeaud herself "went out with the negroes upon the sugar-cane fields, watched them at their work, attended them home, and looked after their food and their comfort, treating them all according to justice and reason. From this moment the most perfect order and obedience prevailed on the plantation."[53] In other words, Bremer's depictions suggest the belief that mistresses could play a significant role at smoothing tensions within the plantation.

In Anselmo Suárez y Romero's "La llegada al ingenio" ("The Arrival at the Sugar Mill"), an unpublished piece about his mother, the writer provides one of the richest portraits we have of the Cuban slaveholding class ideal of paternalism and, more specifically, an illustration of how the compassionate mistress reaffirmed the notion of slavery as a benevolent institution. Remembering how his mother performed her angelic role to perfection—and here the word "performance" acquires a particularly accurate meaning, for it was a performance, even if she believed in what she was doing—Suárez y Romero describes one final interaction between the slaveholder and her slaves.

> I was remembering the last time my mother visited the sugar mill. As if she were a guardian angel, the slaves kneeled before her. Silently, they stood in a group at a distance and for a long time they contemplated her with intense love and religious respect. She had come to the *ingenio* almost every Christmas, and on every trip, her tender, fair, and elevated heart had wiped away many tears. Slaves who were on the stocks were freed thanks to her

> intervention; she had removed the shackles others wore; no sound of whipping would be heard then; marriage ties consecrated clumsy unions, newborns and recent arrivals from Africa were baptized; she ordered the *negrada* [group of slaves] to line up to pray, advised them to act peacefully, went to the infirmary often, prayed next to those who were dying, and before her servants' bodies, she prayed many times, together with other slaves, asking for forgiveness and grace for the souls of the dead. No wonder the slaves looked at her as a heavenly creature and her presence on the plantation was viewed as the sun that in the middle of the sea shines after the storm, or fresh water from a creek found by the travelers in the sand of the desert. She began going to the sugar mill at the height of her youth and beauty; but the last time she visited, old age had already curved her body, though it had not extinguished in her breast the fire of charity. She did what she had always done, gave generously what she had; the black women kissed her thinning hands, made their children who had not met her yet kneel before her, and Ursula, the Carabalí slave, in her seventies, as if my mother were another African and not her mistress, called her "Lugarda" repeatedly, hugging her warmly in her strong arms."[54]

When slave-owning women like the one Suárez described played their role with skill, when they nursed sick slaves and attended to their food and clothing, when they took their obligations seriously, they brought some measure of relief to the nightmarish reality the enslaved population endured. In their position as motherly figures who were moved not by economic interests but by compassion, good mistresses could in principle help lessen the cruelty of slaves' predicament, while also easing slaves' accommodation to their condition. Yet, their involvement could also be smoke and mirrors, their actions obfuscating the cruel destiny of slaves. As Saidiya Hartman reminds us, "Love encourages forgetting, which is intended to wash away the slave's past. Love makes a place for the stranger, . . . it domesticates persons from 'outside of the house,' it assuages the slave's loss of family; it remakes slaveholders as mothers and fathers. Owning persons and claiming kin are one and the same, so love cannot be separated from dispossession or property in persons."[55] Slaveholding women's rationed and sporadic concern for slaves failed to address their basic physical and emotional needs. Mistresses were a useful symbol to the slaveholding community, the reassurance that human touch could override the worst aspects of the institution of slavery. In reality, even under the best circumstances, mistresses' beneficial impact on the lives of the enslaved workers on sugar plantation was limited because of how rarely they visited their properties. Cuban slaveholders, and specifically female slaveholders of sugar mills, were by and large absentee property owners, and their roles as caring figures were less than effective. While their decisions during visits to the plantations could have a transformative impact on the lives of the enslaved people under their control, mistresses' presences in most cases were too brief to create a strong connection or a feeling of mutual obligation between the two groups. Paternalism never had a strong pull among wealthy sugar plantation owners in Cuba, and that weakness is reflected in the many negative portrayals of the *ama* in fiction. It is also true that, in the case of married slave-owning women, we should not overestimate the influence they wielded. As mistresses of sugar mills, they were expected to be in charge of domestic decisions, including those relating to house slaves. The *ama*'s realm was the *casa de vivienda* (the big house). At the plantation, production took precedence over domesticity, the private world becoming secondary to economic considerations. For example, when visiting a sugar mill, Frederika Bremer reported that her hostess deplored her inability to stop the violence against slaves: "'I can not tell you what I have suffered'—she lamented—'nay, indeed, I have been ill for weeks from grief occasioned by the sight of so much flogging, and of the many cruelties, which in many cases, a kind and serious word might have prevented the necessity of!'"[56] But while there were individual women—and men—who objected to the harsh treatment of enslaved people, there is no evidence to suggest that female slaveholders were more critical of the institution of slavery than their male counterparts.

In her study of slaveholding women of the American South, historian Thavolia Glymph questioned the feminist scholarship that came out in the United States in the 1980s. Glymph, challenging the notion of powerless plantation mistresses, concluded that these women indeed were full accomplices in the barbarities committed against the enslaved population.[57] Glymph also provides a phrase that may accurately reflect the Cuban mistress-slave interaction: the "cruelty of indifference."[58] In *Cecilia Valdes*, the writer Cirilo Villaverde left an illuminating example of the ameliorating yet unfulfilled role a mistress could have played because of that detachment. When an enslaved pregnant woman is about to be punished with a *bocabajo* (a whipping inflicted while the victim was lying on the ground, in which a hole had been dug so as not to harm the fetus and future slave), the woman begs for mercy by reminding the overseer that the mistress is her *madrina* (godmother or protector). "Yo' grace not goin' to punish me, my godmother protec' me." The overseer mocks her: "Ha, Ha! You makin' me laugh. The Señora your godmother! Well, tell her to get up out of bed and come to save you from a floggin.' Look, you black devil, lie down and turn over on your belly or I kill you."[59] The ineffectiveness of the mistress, blissfully sleeping while the young woman is about to be punished, is clear.

Women of the slaveholding class lived in contact with slavery from the time they were born: As we have seen in chapter 1, their nurses were often enslaved women who breastfed the white baby at the expense of their own, or who tried to nurse both the master's child and their own at the same time, in which case the two children were called *hermanos de leche* (milk siblings). That close interaction with slaves continued as a white girl grew up. "As soon as a girl begins to babble," the countess of Merlín explained in a letter to French novelist George Sand, "she's given a little girl slave who becomes her playmate, later her maid, and who after a few years obtains her freedom."[60] When the aristocrat visited her family's plantation in 1840, after many years abroad, she rejoiced in receiving the visit of many of the slaves who had served her in her childhood: some had played with her, this one had always carried her in her arms, that one had combed her hair, yet another had sung her songs to help her fall asleep.[61] While the countess of Merlín viewed slavery as a mutually beneficial institution for masters and slaves, the Cuban writer Aurelia del Castillo, a strong abolitionist, held a different view. In her opinion, white women's upbringing made it impossible for them to empathize. For the Camagueyan author, slavery was a moral outrage that diminished the lives of slaves and poisoned from birth the souls of slaveholding women. In 1878, writing from Spain, in a piece she called "The Cuban Woman," Castillo wrote: "even before she becomes accustomed to dozens of voices, her ears already know the words master and slave. When the children's games begin, her playmate is another little girl of the same age. But this girl is black and the color draws a rigid line between them. The black girl finds herself suffering from all the perverse impulses of the other, or maybe it is simply that fleeting malevolence that can be found in children, but she cannot retaliate. And the other knows, even in her innocence, her absolute power, and the former her absolute submission." She concluded: "There is no woman in the civilized world who is born and develops under worse circumstances than the Cuban woman."[62]

Cuban women of the privileged class had to reconcile the notion of slavery as a benevolent institution, on the one hand, and the reality of slave rebellions and enslaved people's constant resistance to their condition, on the other. Signs of slaves' unhappiness were everywhere. Edwin Atkins, an American who owned several plantations near Cienfuegos as slavery was coming to an end in Cuba, wrote about how "two guards with loaded rifles were stationed day and night on either side of the big front door."[63]

And Fredrika Bremer wrote, "The life of the ladies is not cheerful, and scarcely active at all. They seem to me to suffer from the condition of the plantation, which is never free from danger, and which does not allow them to develop at all their more beautiful activity—nay, which even checks their movement. They dare not go out alone—they are afraid of runaway slaves."[64] Statements like this one remind us how difficult it must have been to keep up the pretence that masters and their enslaved workers shared common interests.

CONCLUSION

Examining Cuban slaveholding women's sporadic visits to their plantations offers an opportunity to capture the multiple contradictions of their performance as rulers. Mistresses lived in a patriarchal society that limited their ability to make choices, while also providing them with enormous power over enslaved people's lives. They were the beneficiaries of a brutal economy driven by profits, while their society assigned them the role of compassionate caretakers. In most cases they neither reached the standard of the angelic mistress, devoted to her slaves, nor sank to the level of psychopathic slave drivers. It was within their purview to attempt to make slavery more palatable during their temporary stays on the plantations. But having become desensitized to the plight of their slaves as the result of their upbringing, they were often unable to meet the expectations of the good mistress. More significantly, their condition as absentee landladies undermined the illusion that they were caring mothers who took care of slaves' needs; mistresses' presence at their plantations only served as a reminder of their imminent absence. And perhaps more than anything else, it was the enslaved themselves, when they ran away, when they questioned the masters' justice, when they rebelled against the system, when they refused to play the role of grateful subjects, who shattered the illusion that their bondage was a benevolent institution and the *ama* was a kind, motherly figure.

3

Coffee Plantation Mistresses

As we have seen, slave mistresses seldom visited their sugar mills, and when they did, it was more out of obligation than as a source of enjoyment. They often rushed back to their town residence as soon as they could. Because of the brevity of the family's stay, no serious attempt was made to make the big house comfortable and beautiful. Coffee plantations (*cafetales*) were different: whether or not a *cafetal* was a slaveholder's permanent home, the type of landscape required for growing coffee (with its red earth and striking vegetation) often made for beautiful properties that the owners took great pride in. Coffee plantations sprang up south and east of Havana and northeast of Santiago. They were particularly successful during the first four decades of the nineteenth century, when Cuba was one of the world's leading producers.

For wealthy Havana residents, coffee plantations, worked by slaves and adorned with a rich variety of fruit trees and scented flowers, became status symbols, beautiful getaways where they could receive guests and feel like the European landed aristocracy they were trying to emulate. As Cuban historian Ramiro Guerra explained, the rural property was meant to enhance the owners' social position, and to provide them the satisfaction of feeling like feudal lords. With their coffee plantations located not too far from Havana, but not too close either, families could get there in less than a day, either on horseback or by carriage.[1] For many other owners, in the foothills of Sierra Maestra in the eastern part of the island, and in Artemisa and Vuelta Abajo, in the west, the *cafetal* became their permanent home, which made the planters even more eager to turn their residences into elegant and comfortable living spaces. A sketch by Samuel Hazard captures the pleasing, welcoming environment of a coffee plantation (figure 3.1). Visitors admiringly described their gated entrances with intermittent rows of palm, orange, and banana trees, the colorful fruit one could see everywhere making a striking contrast to the green coffee leaves.[2] The home *(casa de vivienda)*, built of stone and expensive wood, had elegant furniture, chandeliers, paintings, mirrors, and a ballroom, where family and guests gathered for the popular *contradanza* and other kinds of dances. In a letter to a European friend, the countess of Merlín described her visit to Tentativa, one of those beautiful *cafetales* that proclaimed its owners' social standing:

> Several guests who had been invited to spend the day with us arrived, the time flying, divided between walks, music, and dancing, since people from Havana find time to dance at all hours, even when the heat is extreme. At four o'clock we were served an excellent meal in three parts, in other words, on three different tables according to the local custom; the first and second courses in the home's interior galleries, then in the garden filled with greenery surrounding a fountain with running water, the dessert consisted of fruits, delicious sweets, and ice cream, the dancing beginning again and lasting until late into the night, when already tired, filled with happiness and pleasure, I fell asleep on a bed of linen, lace, and red ribbon, the windows open and the moon shining on my face.[3]

The countess's account includes no reference to the presence of slaves or other Black people at the party. Hers is an enthusiastic report of the idiosyncrasies of Cuban culture that a European of her status would find interesting and foreign. But the participation of African-descended people at this gathering, an example of the island's cultural distinctiveness, is undeniable. Slaves would have been the ones cooking and serving the food, the ones preparing the rooms and tables, the ones tending the gardens, and much more. Black freedpeople would almost always have been the ones playing the music that accompanied the dancers into the night, since most Cuban musicians in nineteenth-century Cuba were *hombres libres de color*. Free and enslaved, Black and white, men and women, all contributed to the creation of a society with its own traditions, separate from those of Spain, despite the elite's dismissiveness of the role people of color were playing in that process.

In addition to the *casa de vivienda*, a typical coffee plantation included the overseer's house, stables, coffee dryers, and an outdoor kitchen. It could also include storerooms, an ironing room, a hen house, and a pigeon house.[4] Like sugar mills, *cafetales* required a hospital or infirmary for recently bought slaves, in weak condition after their Atlantic crossing, and for the sick and injured.[5] Also indispensable was a jail or secure room in which to punish the enslaved people who rebelled. A coffee plantation needed a smaller *dotación* (group) of slaves than a plantation with a sugar mill, in many cases fewer than one hundred. The *bohío*, a group of huts lined up in a semi-circular

Figure 3.1. *Cafetal*, in Samuel Hazard, *Cuba with Pen and Pencil* (1871), 334.

fashion, was the enslaved population's living quarters, a more humane arrangement than the characteristic *barracón* (slave barrack) of the sugar mill. But after a wave of slave rebellions in 1825, coffee plantation owners tightened security measures and began locking up their slaves at night, as was commonly done in the *ingenios*. In some cases, a wall was built around the *bohíos*, in an attempt, as Theresa A. Singleton has pointed out in her archaeological study of a *cafetal*, to "other" the enslaved population by concealing slaves' living spaces and creating distance between enslavers and those they controlled.[6]

Mary Gardner Lowell, the traveler from Massachusetts mentioned in chapter 1, visited several Cuban *cafetales* in 1831 and 1832 with her husband and child, and wrote a travel account of her experience. The Lowells were part of an affluent and well-connected New England family and had free entry into the homes of Cuba's wealthy, English-speaking community, a growing sector that included British and North American plantation owners, some of whom had also been slave traders. Ebenezer William Sage and his wife, Hepsey, the Lowells' good friends from Connecticut, owned Santa Ana, a beautiful plantation not far from Matanzas, where the visitors spent time, giving Mary Lowell the opportunity to observe the place and people living there.[7] Following common wisdom among coffee planters, the great house had been built on a hill, the elevation providing both safety and a clear view of slaves' activities. A piazza in front led to a beautiful garden with a rich variety of trees and shrubs that the couple proudly cultivated. Lowell was impressed by the plantation mistress's responsibilities: "Hepsey (Mrs. Sage) . . . occupies herself all the time being obliged to do all her own sewing, to visit the sick negroes & to superintend every domestic arrangement. She knows a great deal about the place every tree upon it & all variety of interests. She has acquired sufficient knowledge of Spanish to converse fluently which is necessary to live here with comfort."[8] Guests and hosts passed their time with dinners and conversation. They visited nearby estates by *quitrín* (a two-wheeled open carriage), and went on horseback-riding excursions that allowed them to enjoy the striking natural beauty of that region. Yet for all their pleasant diversions, the tension between slaveholders and the enslaved could not be ignored.

As soon as they arrived in Cuba, the Lowells had been made aware of the white population's deep fear of slave rebellions; discussions of insurrections on neighboring islands were common in Havana.[9] At their friends' coffee plantation, the mistress herself confirmed those fears when she recounted nervously the story of a rebellion that had taken place only a few years earlier at a nearby plantation, while she and her husband were traveling in the United States. "It is probable both Sage and Hepsey would have been murdered had they not been absent," Lowell wrote. "It began on the estate of Mr. Armitage himself, his wife & three sons and & I don't know how many more were killed. They were extremely indulgent to their blacks & had not the least suspicion of danger . . . The slaves said after killing Mrs. Armitage that it would go against them for they had killed a woman."[10] The palpable threat of revolt had prompted slaveholders like the Sages to take extra precautions. "In the evening," Lowell wrote, "we went to see the negroes dance which is a most peculiar exhibition. Formerly, they were allowed to have this recreation Saturday aft[ernoon] & Sunday but since the insurrection Mr. Sage has forbidden their dancing at any time except before sundown Sunday . . . Mr. Sage shuts all the blacks out of the house at night, indeed, the house itself is a sort of Castle & in his bed room he keep two or three pairs of pistols, guns & swords. Everybody rides armed . . . Mr. S has the noisiest dogs . . . some of the dogs are very savage."[11]

The next planter the Lowells visited was Sarah Jenckes, also an American, who owned a large *cafetal*, with 150 slaves, outside of Havana. A widow, Jenckes was entirely in charge of all financial and management decisions at her plantation. Lowell described her admiringly: "Mrs. Jenckes is a remarkable fine looking old lady, about sixty five or sixty six years of age. She has a high smooth forehead and good features. She dresses in a plain lawn cap with a delicate border & white lawn gown she wears a black lace veil which is sometimes on her shoulders & sometimes drawn over her cap. Her manners are extremely cordial & dignified & one feels at home at once." When the Lowells arrived, the woman planter was in the process of getting twenty new *negros*, recently brought from Africa, ready to work. After they had been fattened for a month, the mistress was confident they would soon be "quite hearty." The newcomers had received new clothes, "blue checked pantaloons & shirts," and new Christian names, now pasted on their shoulders, "their baptism a necessary condition before they could be legally owned"[12] The mistress's role in acculturating her slaves is obvious here. She was the one framing the rules the enslaved people would have to live by from that point on: their new names, religion, clothes, work, schedule, food, housing, and much more. Lowell thought the slaves' living quarters looked comfortable, and she enjoyed her visit to the small building where slaves' children, who were too young to work, lived under the supervision of an older Black woman. In her estimation, Mrs. Jenckes was a good slaveholder. "The slaves here are well fed and taken care of; they all look hearty. Mrs. Jenckes says they have fresh meat every day and plenty of plantain and *funche* [cornmeal, water, and lard]."[13] The final property the travelers visited, thanks to a letter of introduction, was Reserva, a large plantation belonging to Nathaniel Fellowes, a widower from Massachusetts, the owner of several properties and more than four hundred slaves. At the time of the Lowells' stay, Fellowes's sister, Nancy Williams, played the role of mistress of a plantation that Mary Lowell described as a "splendid place." The guest noted the beauty of the house, the striking landscapes painted on the walls, the brilliant polish of the floors, everything looking immaculate, thanks to the work of slaves. The days at Reserva were pleasantly spent sewing, talking, and riding with Mrs. Williams around the plantation, until it was time to dress for dinner. In the evenings, they chatted and listened to Mrs. Williams's daughter play the harp. Mrs. Williams, like many other slaveholding women, tried to create the image of placidity that coffee plantation owners wanted their property to project. In their eyes, their *cafetal* was a beautiful, quiet place where slaves and owners lived untroubled lives, as long as the masters knew how to handle their work force. "The house servants are very good," Lowell recorded, "and Mrs. Williams expressed her surprise at hearing of the wretched set upon other states I had visited, she said she considered the good servants one of the greatest advantages of living upon the island. Of course they require a steady hand and superintendence but when you have established your authority but little discipline is necessary."[14]

Slaveholders, both male and female, played a direct, personal role in the ultimately unattainable goal of achieving total control of the slave population by interfering with their everyday lives—in terms of their material conditions, the food they were fed, the clothes they received, the homes they inhabited, the jobs they were assigned, their religious and cultural practices, and what they were allowed to do in their free time. Working conditions at coffee plantations were less brutal than those endured at sugar mills (since picking coffee beans was easier than cutting cane and didn't require work shifts during nights, as sugar did), but idleness was not allowed. Slaveholders believed that keeping the enslaved work force occupied at all time reduced the threat of revolts, and they found plenty of tasks for slaves to perform, including doing the upkeep of the plantation, taking care of the garden, and building paths and roads.[15] The slaveholding class hoped that their control over slaves' activities and material life, along with psychological pressure to make slaves accept their subjugated status, would be sufficient to maintain order, but the general feeling of insecurity that permeated life on the Cuban plantation landscape indicates that the masters knew their authority was tenuous.[16] Whether by joining organized rebellions, or by creating tight-knit communities that helped them maintain their religion, music, dances, cultural values, and sense of identity, the enslaved fought back. In investigating the power struggle between slaveholders and slaves, Manuel Barcia has pointed out, we should look not only for major rebellions, but also for small acts of insubordination, such as the concealment of potential weapons, harboring of runaways, and so forth.[17] The master class preferred not to admit to any tension between themselves and the enslaved population, as that would imply a need to address the unjust social structure that allowed slaveholders to live in comfort. They were particularly defensive of the institution of slavery when discussing it with foreigners, as illustrated in Mary Peabody Mann's semifictional account of life on a *cafetal.*

In 1832, the same year Mary Gardner Lowell left the island, another female American writer, Mary Peabody, along with her sister Sophia, arrived for what would be a one-and-one-half-year stay at a coffee plantation, not far from Havana, where the sisters would work as tutors for the Morrells, a Cuban family. The Peabody sisters were part of New England's intellectual elite, socializing with the likes of Margaret Fuller, Ralph Waldo Emerson, and Henry Thoreau. After returning home, Mary Peabody married the educator Horace Mann, and Sophia became the wife of Nathaniel Hawthorne. While not ignorant of the impact of slavery, which was very much alive in the southern states of their own country, the two young women had never experienced life on a slave plantation before. The horror of what they saw inspired Mary to write *Juanita: A Romance of Real Life in Cuba Fifty Years Ago* (1887). The book was published with the disclaimer that the characters were all fictional, yet the author waited to publish it until the death of the family members she wrote about. According to Mary's elder sister, Elizabeth Peabody, the novel reflected what Mary "had seen and known of real life in Cuba, woven into work of art."[18] The book's most notable characters are the mistress (a Cuban woman named Isabella married to a Spanish aristocrat) and her school friend, Helen Wentworth (an American, based on Peabody herself and the one portrayed as having a moral compass thanks to her Puritan background). Mary Peabody Mann wrote, "Helen Wentworth was a Massachusetts girl, . . . nurtured upon the trials, sacrifices, and conquests of the early Pilgrim history, which has made New England what it is. Helen's more puritanical manners and higher culture had developed a superior nature, which even a French-boarding school could not fritter away."[19] Isabella, in contrast, while portrayed as above the average Cuban woman because of her US education, lacked her friend's principled views. When the two friends meet in Cuba after years apart, the American visitor is stunned by the coffee plantation's beauty. The delicious climate, the perfume of roses in the air, the sound of the fountain, and the thoughtful design of the piazza and gardens surrounding the house make Helen feel as though she is "in the very gates of Paradise."[20] Yet soon that image falls apart, as she becomes aware of the physical violence and inhumane living conditions that the plantation's enslaved population has to endure. When she confronts her friend, the plantation mistress acknowledges the horrors of slavery, but she defends the need for such treatment with an argument many slaveholding women would have supported: "[Slaves] must feel there is an inexorable power over them, or they would kill us all. The most faithful are not to be trusted in extremity. How can we expect them to be faithful if they see a chance of liberty for themselves? They might not take into account the retribution that would come upon them. Oh dear Helen, I felt as you do when I first came home, but I have resigned myself to necessity. What else can women do? All I can do is to be as good a mistress as I know how, make no unreasonable requisitions, and bear all the evils that I see."[21] Being a good mistress, for Isabella, means visiting sick slaves in the hospital and attending personally to their rations. It means overseeing the making of slaves' clothes three months a year and, in general, being a benevolent influence on the life of the *cafetal*—in other words, making compassionate gestures without ever disturbing the status quo. Like many other female plantation owners, raised without having domestic responsibilities, Isabella is an incompetent manager and leaves many of those duties to a female slave, the mistress's hopelessness a reminder that rivalry between women did not always have a sexual dimension. When her American friend questions the rude behavior of Camilla, the household's head slave, and asks Isabella why she puts up with her, the mistress replies:

> Because she knows how to do everything, and I cannot keep house without her. That she knows this is my misfortune. She has a true genius for organization, and is accomplished in every household art. She has her corps of sweepers, house-washers, dish-washers, laundry-women, errand boys. She is the queen of pastry cooks. In that little pantry from which you see her emerge, she performs miracles of that sort. It is a small place, but everything in it is kept in neat order, and out of it come the rarest viands, cakes, custards, tarts, sweetmeats, candied fruits, and all the devices of French and Spanish cooking. She can always judge of the quantity of food to be provided for any occasion, and has her reserved forces for an emergency—saves all her nice scraps for the hospital, and never is so completely in her element as when there is too much to do.[22]

Though a fictional account, this exchange reflects a reality in the life of a plantation. Mistresses and house slaves were not equally qualified to manage a household. Surrounded by slaves since they were children, wealthy women were not taught to be resourceful and self-reliant. It is likely that their weakness in household matters provided enslaved women some room to negotiate their living conditions. Many female slave owners relied on their slaves for the smooth functioning of their domestic life, and thus their ability to perform competently their role as mistress was dependent on their slaves' skills as cooks, washers, housemaids, and so on. The difference in competence, when it came to domestic matters, may have worked to equalize to a small degree the mistress-slave interaction.

As we have seen, American travelers such as Mary Gardner Lowell and Mary Peabody Mann naturally gravitated to plantation owners from the United States. There were also British and Germans among the plantation owners, but the largest contingent of foreign coffee growers were the French émigrés. France had occupied the western half of Hispaniola since the mid-seventeenth century and had turned Saint Domingue into a thriving coffee plantation society. In the late 1700s and early 1800s, French property owners, as well as artisans, businessmen, and people of all sorts fled the revolution that put an end to slavery in Haiti. Bringing with them what little they could save, including when possible their slaves, they resettled in eastern Cuba. Many found in Santiago, Guantánamo, and other vicinities a hospitable environment in which to start over: They opened art, music, dance, and sewing schools, and helped the local economy thrive. Those who could afford to do so bought land, mostly in the foothills of Sierra Maestra, an ideal area, because of its altitude and humidity, and resolutely established new coffee plantations. Thanks to the spectacular increase in coffee prices in the early years of the nineteenth century, they once again accumulated enormous fortunes.

Their homes, nestled in the mountains, were comfortable and refined: they had fireplaces and libraries, as well as music rooms, where hired musicians, usually free Black men, played popular tunes. As Marta Lora Alvarez has observed, using the area's topography wisely—its creeks, rivers, and streams—the French were able to create a physical environment that was practical for their business needs, as well as beautiful.[23]

American traveler Samuel Hazard found the landscape of the *cafetales* in Sierra Maestra stunning. In his writing he attempted to capture the habitat's Romantic beauty with descriptions of the impressive mountains, hidden valleys, mossy rocks, strange trees, beautiful ferns, and luxuriant vegetation that served as the natural backdrop for this community.[24] The large size of the French population in eastern Cuba allowed the group to maintain a distinct identity: They continued to speak French throughout their lives, married within the community, served as godparents to each other's children, and provided help and security for one another. Their shared loyalty to their ancestral mother country strengthened their ties in the new environment, but it also made them vulnerable to the political ups and downs of the relationship between the Spanish and French governments. During Napoleon's invasion of the Peninsula, French settlers were expelled from the Spanish colonies in retaliation, many of them resettling permanently or temporarily in New Orleans, by then already part of the United States, but a city that had maintained a strong French flavor.[25] That was the case in María Luisa Girard's family.

María Luisa Girard grew up in a French-speaking family that had moved to eastern Cuba from Saint Domingue after losing their plantations to Haiti's revolution. In 1809, when she was two years old, her family was forced to relocate to New Orleans. Ten years later, the family returned to Cuba, where they prospered as coffee plantation owners in Sierra Maestra.[26] As Cuban historian Olga Portuondo Zúñiga has pointed out in her biographical study, María Luisa Girard grew up surrounded by slaves under the watchful eye of her mother, a well-educated woman, who taught her daughter to be attentive not only to domestic matters but also to the coffee crops and the work of the slaves. In 1830, María Luisa married Domingo de Heredia, a wealthy coffee plantation owner, also from Saint Domingue, a widower twenty years her senior who credited his success to the strict order and discipline he imposed on his slaves. Ultraconservative, he demanded protection from the colonial government's against potential fugitive slaves' attacks. Like many members of the Creole bourgeoisie during this period, Heredia supported the restoration of King Ferdinand VII and the monarch's defense of absolutism and free trade, a winning formula for the planter class. María Luisa and Domingo embraced the nineteenth-century paternalistic ideal of slavery and liked to think of themselves as enlightened figures who ruled over helpless enslaved men and women with a benevolent yet firm hand. They despised abolitionists and defended the preservation of slavery as the best arrangement to keep the African population working and living an orderly existence.[27] In her letters to relatives, Portuondo records, María Luisa proudly claimed "how much her slaves loved her."[28] The couple lived and raised their children at La Fortuna, one of their coffee plantations, described by María Luisa as "her paradise." For the masters, it was indeed paradisiacal. A luscious garden surrounded the beautifully furnished house with its well-stocked library and music room. Using the finest china, they served succulent and abundant meals accompanied by exquisite wines and gathered around the grand piano for musical evenings. There were horse stables, a mill, storage for coffee and other crops, a hospital, as well as the *bohíos* that housed the more than one hundred slaves that worked there. In a small chapel the slave owners celebrated mass, occasionally also attended by slaves who were expected to be inspired by the liturgy and the music. The family socialized with other French-speaking neighbors and relatives, and, like many of their friends, sent their sons and daughters to be educated in France.

Jean Baptiste Rosamond de Beauvallon, the Frenchman born on the island of Guadeloupe mentioned in chapter 1, who in 1841 and 1842 crisscrossed Cuba by horse, visited the Heredia-Girard family *cafetal* and other members of the French community in the mountains northeast of Santiago. Beauvallon got along well with the Cuban elite. Like many of them, he viewed himself as an enlightened modern man, who appreciated technological innovations while also being opposed to the abolition of slavery. The French immigrant community from Saint Domingue had his utmost admiration: they had tamed the wilderness of Sierra Maestra, they had remade their lives and rebuilt their fortunes, without giving up their French identity and culture. Before arriving at María Luisa Girard's home, Beauvallon stopped at Saint-Jules, a coffee plantation belonging to the Dutocq family, which included thirty-nine slaves. He admired Madame's ebony dining table with its centerpiece of European flowers grown in her garden. He admired even more her own refinement and ability to converse about Lamartine, Victor Hugo, and other French writers. "Our kind hostess playfully analyzed the work of the most current writers," he wrote.[29] He then rode to La Fortuna, the large Heredia-Girard coffee plantation atop the mountain, where he found the mistress of the house in her living room, surrounded by her family. Everything exuded an air of elegance, luxury, and comfort.[30] In honor of the French guest, the family had organized a social gathering that gave him the opportunity once again to praise the beauty and refinement of the French community, including all the beautiful girls and young women—"the mountain's daughters," as he called them—in pink or white dresses and, thanks to their mothers, equipped with a solid musical, literary, and religious education.[31] In the morning, he observed with satisfaction one of María Luisa Girard's daughters, as she, "overcoming her youthful delicacy," served slave children their rations, proof that she had been taught her role as a Christian mistress.[32]

Business matters forced María Luisa Girard's husband to take frequent trips, and she became accustomed to making decisions herself about the household and the plantations. When her husband died, she continued to be in charge of the family's properties.[33] Girard liked to think of herself as a magnanimous mistress who was willing to overlook her slaves' deficiencies. When visiting her plantations, she brought the slaves small presents such as meat, cigars, and wine, and enjoyed their demonstrations of humble devotion, like kissing her hand or kneeling before her. In a letter to her son, who was studying in France, she told him how during the Christmas holiday, she had distributed clothing, especially among those slaves who bore the family's last name.[34] She had also given out an abundant ration of salt, handkerchiefs, hats for the children, coins, and a gourd for each mother of a child.[35] She proudly took credit[36] for the survival of the more than two hundred slaves who had been born in her properties during her thirty years as mistress.[37]

Clare Bonne, another French Creole who moved to Santiago after the Haitian revolution, belonged to a lower class than Girard, but she illustrates the opportunities for social mobility that slave ownership could provide white women. Cuban historian Sajay Fajardo has carefully traced Bonne's life after her arrival in Cuba without wealth or connections. Remaining legally unmarried until right before her partner died, she lived and raised a large and tight-knit family with a man who was a jeweler, the couple taking financial advantage of the various waves of immigrants settling in Santiago in the early 1800s, and the growing consumer demands that came with prosperity. She bought and managed houses until she accumulated enough capital to buy *cafetales* worked by slaves, at a time when coffee prices were high and the plantation economy became consolidated. Their slaveholding status allowed her and her family to move up the social ladder. Like many other Haiti refugees, Clare Bonne continued to speak French throughout her life.[38]

Frederica Bremer, the Swedish traveler mentioned in chapter 2, left a description of a yet another female French planter. In May 1852, at the coffee plantation Concordia, Bremer encountered Señora Carrera, an escapee from Saint Domingue and the widow of a Spanish aristocrat. She was, the traveler explained, "one of those beautiful maternal women, who are a blessing in all the countries of the world, and who are able, at least for a moment, to remove even from slavery its oppressive fetters, and to allow the slaves to forget them." Bremer witnessed and recorded approvingly slaves' happiness when the lady of the plantation returned, her concern for the sick, how she sent them food and other special treats, slave children's ease when playing around her, and her warm greetings to the adults.[39]

Hippolyte Piron, a traveler discussed in chapter 1 whose family, like Girard's and Carrera's, had made a fortune in eastern Cuba by growing coffee, had a less benign view of this community of slaveholders. In his travelogue, he tells the haunting story of a wealthy and sadistic slaveholder, identified only as Madame X, who subjected her slaves to horrendous punishments and enjoyed torturing them with hot coals. Envious of a slave woman's beautiful teeth, Madame X pulled them out with pincers and tried in vain to place them in her own gums. Her slaves dared not look for another owner out of fear of repercussions.[40] After traveling all over the countryside, Piron concluded that slavery in rural Cuba was a sad spectacle, among other reasons, because of the plantations' remoteness. The master had complete control, with no need to explain anything to anyone, and it was difficult, practically impossible, for enslaved people to find a *síndico* (government official appointed as slave representative) to advocate for them.[41] In his opinion, most slaves hated their masters, but there was little they could do, other than try to make a dangerous escape to a *palenque*, a refuge deep in the woods where runaways hid. While the law mandated that masters and mistresses were to provide clothing for enslaved men, women, and children twice a year—each man was to receive pants, a shirt, a felt hat, a jacket, and a blanket; each woman a dress, kerchief, hat, jacket, and blanket[42]—Piron denounced their failure to fulfill this obligation and the white women's hypocrisy. Observing the sad state of slaves' clothes, dirty, ragged, or nonexistent, with children of both sexes running around naked until the age of twelve, he wrote: "The white ladies' and young *señoritas'* modesty is in no way offended by this custom dating to the happy days of Adam and Eve [*paraíso terrenal*]; they made themselves be served by these *negritos* with the most admirable coolness."[43]

In 1864, trying to escape the summer heat, Walter Goodman, the British artist and traveler introduced in chapter 1, accepted an invitation to visit a coffee plantation. Joining the family of a wealthy planter, Goodman left Santiago with the rest of the party before the sun came up, the men riding on horses, the domestic slaves with the luggage on mules and carts drawn by oxen, and the ladies and children traveling by *quitrín*. After an arduous day traveling over remote roads, they arrived at the *cafetal*, a scene of orange and mangrove groves, pineapples, plantains, and all sorts of plants creating a beautiful effect. Family and guests were offered a bath and provided with fresh clothes and coffee before a savory dinner of chicken, cod, cabbage, stewed goat, bacon, yam, preserves, and wine, followed by cigars.

Having finished their work, the field slaves had to come to request their master's blessing, under the watchful stare of the overseer holding a whip. The next morning, Goodman went on a stroll with the planter and witnessed the flogging of a young female slave, the mother of a five-month-old baby, before she was consigned to solitary confinement in a dark room, as punishment for being "ungovernable" and "insubordinate."[44] After observing slaves hard at work picking coffee berries, the men went back to the house for breakfast, so as to not keep the ladies—who had not been involved in any of the inspection activities, and therefore had avoided witnessing the flogging—waiting. When they were done with breakfast, they brought hammocks to a nearby stream and rested while enjoying nature's beauty.[45] Goodman's anecdote is significant in that it reveals how white women were sheltered from some of the more wrenching aspects of slavery. Defined as they were by their domestic environment, as in this case, the wife and daughters of the plantation owner were not expected to make the rounds and inspect the workings of their estate. They could avoid seeing and confronting the reality of slaves' living conditions; their delicacy did not have to be offended by the sight of the lashing of a young mother. They could wait for the men to come back from all that, have breakfast, and then lie down on a hammock and enjoy the beautiful landscape.

CONCLUSION

During the first four decades of the nineteenth century, Cuba became the top coffee producer in the world, which created enormous wealth for the planter class, particularly near Havana, in the western part of the island, and in Sierra Maestra on the eastern side. The beautiful green vegetation and red earth surrounding coffee plantations made them status symbols for their owners, who often turned them into their permanent homes and proudly opened them up to visitors. Life for the enslaved population was not as brutal here as it was on a sugar plantation, allowing the planter class more easily to imagine themselves as benevolent rulers of a utopian community. Women like María Luisa Girard spent years managing their plantations and making economic decisions that would benefit them and their descendants. Living on site, coffee plantation mistresses had both the opportunity and power to play a significant role in setting the cultural and social norms for their slaves. Ultimately, the contrast between the refined, luxurious lives the masters enjoyed and the hardships the enslaved population endured made *cafetales* a symbol of the ugliness of slavery, and a reminder of female slaveholders' steadfast determination to retain their wealth and power at the expense of other human beings' liberty.

4

"I Bequeath"

Slaveholding Women's Wills

In 1839, María Luisa Dinet, an affluent elderly woman who lived in Santiago de Cuba, made her will in the presence of her lawyer. As was customary, the document began with a statement affirming her status as the legitimate daughter of her already deceased parents; that she was of sound mind despite her physical infirmity; her faith in the Catholic religion, and her trust in the Almighty to forgive her sins. Doña María Luisa Dinet had been born in the French colony of Saint Domingue and had inherited considerable wealth from her parents.[1] By 1839 she was ready to identify the heirs to her property, a decision fully in her hands, given that she was single and without direct descendants. Her estate included two houses in Santiago de Cuba, a *colgadizo* (a small house with a pent roof), and two coffee plantations, all of them free of debt or mortgages, along with seventeen slaves. She was owed 21,820 pesos, and she owned jewelry, furniture, and clothing, which was stored in a chest. Dinet chose to leave 6,000 pesos to her nephew don Pedro Merlé, as a sign of affection and to thank him for unspecified services; a smaller amount, 2,000 pesos, to don Augusto Rebié, another nephew, also as a sign of gratitude. These two nephews were to receive all her furniture, silver and gold jewelry, and the money she was owed. As her lawyer would inform them when the time came, she left 1,000 pesos to each of her two brothers, both residents of New Orleans, and 2,000 pesos to her sister. Her nephew, don Juan Bautista Dení (the last name spelled in various ways throughout the will), would receive 600 pesos, and another nephew, Juan Vidox Bayeur, 100 pesos. The woman taking care of her in her sickness was left 200 pesos. Dinet also stipulated that after her death the *negrita* Cristina, who was her slave Martina's daughter, as well as two other young slaves, named Carlos and Anita, and the *mulatico* Juan Bautista Alonso should all be set free, but that they should continue to work for her nephews until they turned twenty-five or married, at which time they should get their manumission papers. Those were just the preliminaries. María Luisa Dinet left most of her wealth to her two young nieces so that, as she put it, they would enjoy it with God's blessing and in her name. As the girls were still minors, Dinet appointed one of her nephews, whom she trusted, as the executor, and "for powerful reasons [*por razones ponderosas*]" explicitly excluded the girls' father from any interference. She clarified in her will that the *mulato* Felipe, who had worked for her as a handyman, belonged not to her but to one of her brothers in New Orleans, and that her brother should decide what to do "about his fate." And finally, she declared *coartados* ("allowed" to buy their own freedom gradually) her slaves Silvestre and Agustina, in acknowledgment of their faithfulness and good services.[2]

Nineteenth-century wills are rich documentary sources that help us better understand Cuban women's lives and their world.[3] In the case of María Luisa Dinet, her will reveals, first of all, that she lived in a tight-knit community where most people close to her had a French last name—Dinet, Merlé, Rabié, Vidox, Bayeur. At the signing of her will, in addition to the lawyer, two Spanish and French interpreters (*inteligentes en el idioma castellano y francés*) were present—a reminder that despite many years residing in Cuba, Dinet continued to belong to a French-speaking community. Second, the will shows that Dinet was very much in charge of her own finances and the fate of her slaves. Under Spanish law, women over twenty-five who were single or widowed were "allowed to buy, sell, rent, inherit or bequeath property of all kinds. They could lend and borrow money, act as administrators of estates and appear as witnesses, except in the case of wills."[4] Married women also had the rights to own property and to bequeath their wealth, but they needed their husbands' permission to conduct their legal affairs. In other words, a married woman's husband had legal control of her possessions, including the jointly owned *bienes gananciales* (property acquired during a couple's married life). As a woman who never married, Dinet learned to take care of her own affairs, and she seems to have managed her estate competently. She made her own business decisions, such as lending money, knew the exact amount of money owed to her, and had incurred no debts. She wrote a remarkably specific will without the guidance of male relatives. Her father was dead, and her brothers lived far away in New Orleans. And she made her wishes clear, as illustrated by the stipulation blocking her nieces' father from having access to the inheritance. Like most slave owners in her society, Dinet considered freedom not a right but a special gift that she might or might not grant her slaves. There is an interesting parallel between the manner in which she treats her relatives and her slaves. In both cases, those who have been loyal to her get a reward: for her family members, it is material wealth, for her slaves a *coartación* or a letter of manumission, and in both cases, she considers the gift a magnanimous gesture on her part. When granting freedom to some of her young slaves, she specified that they should continue to work for one of her relatives until they became adults, a decision that, while perhaps stemming from a desire to protect them, raises questions. Maintaining their servitude to the Dinet family guaranteed that the young slaves would be fed and sheltered, but it also provided unpaid workers to her relatives for a number of years. Delaying freedom for the young slaves might have placed them in a vulnerable position; many things could have happened before they reached adulthood. And did the temporary owners relinquish their power in due course? Did they honor Dinet's will and eventually present the slaves with their letters of manumission? We do not know the answer.

Nineteenth-century wills were detailed, complex documents, both formulaic and personal, which provided women, even those without much power, a chance to declare their will loudly and clearly. The phrases "I dispose and order" (*dispongo y mando*), and "it is my will" (*es mi voluntad*) are used over and over throughout the documents. The women's final wishes of what to do with their property had enormous impact on the lives of the enslaved population, as the wills always included instructions on the fate of the men, women, and children under the women's control. The implementation of a mistress's will could have a negative impact—for example, when the procedure resulted in a new master or mistress, thus separating slaves from their friends and relatives, a familiar neighborhood, or an occupation. Or it could have positive consequences. The documents might leave instructions on how certain servants should be *coartados* for a reasonable price, making buying their own freedom a real possibility for slaves, or, in a best case scenario, they might be granted their letter of manumission, which would end their status as slaves. (Few women, however, other than very wealthy owners, considered the latter possibility.)

All wills began with personal information about the signer. The women's social respectability was made clear from the start with their title as *doñas*, a term not applied to those of African descent or those born outside a marriage sanctioned by the church. Wills recorded a myriad of autobiographical facts, including the women's parents' names; whether they were legitimate or illegitimate daughters; the place where they were born and their place of current residence; their civil status as married, single, or widowed; and whether they had offspring. Widows and single women had the freedom (even more if they had no direct descendants) to choose anyone they wanted—such as friends or distant relatives—to inherit their property.

Common reasons listed to meet with the lawyer to write their testament included feeling feeble (*algo achacosa*) and getting old, but it was necessary to make clear that they were sane and mentally capable. As Elena Ducté, a woman from Santiago de Cuba, declared in her will in 1838, she was "somewhat feeble and of advanced age, but fully sane, with intact memory and natural discernment."[5]

Next came the women's obligatory declaration of devotion to the Catholic Church, their belief in the mystery of the Holy Trinity, and their hope that María Santísima would intercede for them and that God would be compassionate and accept them into heaven. As was mandatory, all had to leave money to the church for three obligatory masses for their souls and the three *mandas* (taxes) to pay for them. Many of the women left additional money to the church, the amount depending on their assets. In 1804, the countess of Jaruco, who was immensely wealthy and clearly convinced that she could buy her way into heaven, left instructions and money for no fewer than three thousand masses to be said for her soul, as well as many others for the souls of her parents and other relatives.[6] In 1814 Bernarda de Arango left a provision for her chaplains with the order that they celebrate masses on special days, such as her relatives' birthdays and death anniversaries.[7] Decades later, on January 1, 1871, María del Carmen Sotolengo Alfaro of Havana left money for the traditional three masses for the soul, and the mandatory *mandas*, but also left money for thirty additional masses for San Gregorio.[8]

Specifying what kind of shroud and burial they wanted provided women with another opportunity to exert some level of control. In 1818, María Caridad Méndez of Santiago de Cuba, who identified herself as a *morena libre* (free Black woman), asked to be buried in her parish, wearing a humble shroud, the priest carrying a high cross and wearing a golden cape and escorted by eight attendants.[9] In 1852, Josefa Reyna, a Havana resident, chose to be buried wearing the habit of Our Lady of Mercy.[10]

If the women were married, their wills provided specific information about the property they and their husbands had each contributed to their marriage and what they owned together. In 1814, Barbara María Pérez's husband declared that when the couple were married, neither one had contributed anything, but that during their married life in Santiago de Cuba they acquired the house where they lived, with its corresponding plot, which included a *colgadizo*, where they had a bakery. They also jointly owned a slave named Juana de Dios and her two-year-old daughter named Margarita, as well as the domestic utensils required for a household.[11] María Caridad Méndez, a free woman of color from Santiago de Cuba, stated that she had not contributed any property to her marriage, and that her husband, Andrés

Méndez—also a free person of color, with whom she was *ritualmente casada* (in a marriage sanctioned by the church)—had contributed six mules and a slave named José Trinidad. The property acquired during their marriage included a *colgadizo*; four additional slaves (named Francisco, Manuel, Antonio, and Rafael), all of whom worked with her husband on the family's small tobacco plantation; as well as a pair of oxen, five cows, and several horses. Spanish law stipulated that a "person could dispose of one-fifth of his or her property freely; the other four-fifths had to be divided among the legitimate heirs, with children of both sexes receiving equal shares from both parents."[12] Accordingly, Méndez appointed her husband as her executor and left all her property to her legitimate son Carlos, except for "the fifth" (one-fifth of her assets), which she left to her illegitimate daughter, Ysadora, from a previous relationship.[13]

Doña María Teresa Isabel Gomée, originally from Germany, had married a Frenchman and moved to Saint Domingue, before settling in Cuba. She declared that she and her husband had both contributed assets to their marriage, but that all had been "lost as result of the revolutions in the country where they lived."[14] In 1846, she declared as her only property a female slave and the woman's three children.[15] In 1852, Josefa Reyna, a Havana resident, stated that when she was married, her husband received 1,244 pesos in cash. She also contributed a house on San Nicolás Street, where the couple lived, as well as rent from various properties in Cuba and in Spain that she had inherited, in addition to her clothing and items of personal use. She also owned a Creole slave named Serafio. Her husband had contributed a slave named Francisco Delgado, valued at 544 pesos. By the time Josefa Reyna made her will, the couple had acquired an inn on Dragones Street and had approximately 1,500 pesos as capital.[16] María del Rosario González y Mildres, from Guanabacoa, a widow and the mother of three children, declared that when she married, she had not contributed any sort of property to the partnership. When she made her will in 1862, by which time she was a widow, she owned agricultural land (*tierra de labor*) in San Antonio de los Baños, which she rented; a house, which she also rented; and a forty-year-old slave, Rafael Congo, who was a *coartado*, his price fixed at 400 pesos.[17]

Other information the women's wills provide includes the money they owed or that was owed to them, with the terms worded more vaguely, the lower the women's economic stratum. María Caridad Méndez, the free Black woman from Santiago already mentioned, recorded that she and her husband owed their slaves 180 pesos. How could that be? Most likely, their slaves were hired out to other people and received wages, which they had to split with their master and mistress, and the owners must have borrowed money from their slaves for some unspecified expense.[18]

Nineteenth-century women's wills also offer glimpses of women's material culture, often listing specific objects they owned (such as lamps, china, and silver) in addition to their more substantial properties. A woman of modest means, such as Caridad Méndez, listed among her possessions a gold rosary, two clasps also made out of gold, and two silver clasps.[19] María de los Angeles Rodríguez Gálvez, from Santiago de Cuba but living in Madrid and married to a Basque man, listed among her possessions five houses in Regla; a warehouse to store sugar in the harbor of Areas de Canalí, which she co-owned with another woman; 66 acres of land near Cárdenas; furniture; and other items including jewelry, a silver liquor decanter with twenty-four crystal glasses, a set of silver cruets and tray, two silver sauce dishes, two silver basins and two pitchers of the same material, a silver inkstand, a silver chamber pot, and a silver spittoon. She also mentioned three dozen pieces of silver cutlery, other objects she "failed to remember," as well as an unspecified number of slaves. She ordered that all her property be appraised for auction, with the proceeds divided among her children at her death.[20] In 1864 in Havana, Josefa Rodríguez Morilla listed among her possessions her jewelry, silver spoons, forks, chandeliers, earrings, rings, a grandfather clock, two gold wristwatches, and a gold chain.[21]

In most cases, wills show how married couples worked together to build assets and to increase the value of their belongings, including their slaves. But they could also reflect fractured marriages and how, at times, slaves got caught in the middle of a rancorous family dispute, for better or worse. Matías Bernal, who died in Santiago in 1830, left a will that excluded his estranged wife. According to his account, his mother-in-law and wife had for years taken advantage of him. With the intention of obstructing his chances of earning money, he claimed, the two women had rented out the family slave, the *mulato* Felipe, for 70 pesos per year, so that the master would not benefit from his work, and the mother and daughter kept all the money that Felipe made. In response, in his will, Bernal freed most of his slaves, including his wife's personal slave, and provided 200 pesos to help the others get their freedom. In addition to their manumission papers, the slaves Caridad, María de la Luz, and Dolores *la Conguita* (the Congolese) were to receive all the furniture in the house belonging to him. Bernal urged his executors to proceed quickly on this matter, before the furniture got stolen or deteriorated with the delay. Matías Beltrán's actions to emancipate his slaves seem to have been inspired both by personal sympathy for some of his slaves, and by his desire to take revenge against his wife. They were not the result of having reached a critical view on the institution of slavery: the money he left for his nephews, nieces, and friends included 300 pesos for his *comadre* (a term meaning "female neighbor or friend"; it can also refer to the godmother of one's child), doña Josefa Teran, so that she could buy a slave "to serve her while she lives, her children not having any rights to the slave whatsoever, it being my object that she can keep her without having to sell her."[22]

Just like men's wills, the wills of women provided them with a chance to shape and reshape the world they were leaving behind, and many wanted to set conditions on their heirs before they were allowed to receive their inheritance. The countess of Jaruco left a generous dowry to her two nieces so that they could "marry decently"—but only if their father, the marquis of Cárdenas, whom she charged with overseeing that the girls made "advantageous alliances in accordance to their birth," approved of and consented to the girls' choices.[23] And María de los Angeles Rodríguez Gálvez stated: "It is my will that if any of my legitimate children, sons-in-laws, and grandchildren, or any other person interested in my inheritance or part of it tries to challenge my will or litigate to put in a claim, if they are one of the heirs, simply by this action their corresponding inheritance be lowered by a third, the amount left added to the inheritance of the other heirs, and if they are a legatee, they would lose the bequest in its entirety, which will be equally distributed among the other legatees in equal parts."[24]

Historian Marissa Fuentes, when discussing wills in eighteenth-century Barbados, has pointed out that white women "left wealth in the form of slaves and their children to consolidate the financial stability of their relatives."[25] That was also the case in nineteenth-century Cuba. In accordance with a society that reduced members of the enslaved population to valuable objects, mistresses used them in their wills to reward and benefit friends, relatives, and favorite members of the church. María de los Angeles Rodríguez Gálvez, conforming to her society's formality when referring to a white person, even a child, ordered that her slave Francisca, who was in the service of her granddaughter, doña Susana Benítez, should continue in that position until the girl reached twenty-five years of age, at which point Francisca should get her manumission papers.[26] And in 1814, María Bernarda de Arango of Havana left 300 pesos to the reverend Fray Francisco Rodríguez so he could buy a slave.[27]

Women's testaments provide glimpses of the relationship between *amas* (mistresses) and the enslaved men, women, and children whose lives they controlled. Writing a will was the best opportunity slaveholding women had to reward or punish their slaves depending on how loyal or disloyal they felt the slaves had been. Their decisions reveal how mistresses could and did use their final wishes to reward slaves they considered faithful (for example, by allowing them to be sold for a fixed amount—the lower the price, the easier it would be for a slave to buy his or her freedom—or even by granting them freedom) while leaving the rest in captivity.[28] The wills of female slaveholders also provide occasional examples of the warm personal relations that at times existed between mistresses and slaves. Even if the relationship was characterized by tremendously uneven power, the documents help us trace those patterns of affection, those emotional exchanges that, as historian Susan Broomhall has observed, while analyzing the master/servant personal interaction in medieval Europe, are so hard to locate.[29] There were times when mistresses took this opportunity to leave small tokens of endearment—a piece of clothing or a few coins to a favorite slave—or, on rare occasions, to provide them with a more generous legacy, such as a small house. Most often, slaves did not receive gifts but were themselves gifted to a friend or relative of the signatory. The wide range of decisions, thoughtful, capricious, and indifferent, reflected the complex and wide range of personal relations between mistresses and the enslaved in nineteenth-century Cuba.

We will never fully understand the many complicit gestures, favors, and acts of loyalty slaves had to display to earn their mistresses' sympathies. As Cuban historian Oilda Hevia Lanier has pointed out, behind every concession of freedom exists a complex story the legal document failed to capture.[30] The same is true for the stories of slaves left in bondage and their daily acts of rebellion that put them at odds with their masters or mistresses. Slaves who had the opportunity to be perceived as loyal, faithful, affectionate, and useful—those who were in contact with their owners regularly enough to form personal ties—were the ones most likely to be set free or to receive other testimonies of appreciation. Domestic slaves, because of their greater chances of personal interaction, were the ones who benefited the most from their mistresses' will. Personal maids, cooks, and nurses were more likely to be acculturated and to have performed valuable services that mistresses would want to reward. They had a better opportunity to be viewed as individuals, and the testaments often mention them in a more familiar, concrete manner, by name and occupation, while plantation slaves tend to be identified more vaguely and by their ethnic marker, as Carabalí, Congo, Mandinga, Lucumí, Ibo, and so on.[31]

In 1789 Inés González de Carbajal, a resident of Havana, ordered in her will that two slaves, named Fermín and María Dolores, should be set free. She also favored four loyal slaves with *coartaciones*, ranging—depending on how close she felt to each of them, we can presume—between 150 and 300 pesos.[32] In 1814, Maria Bernarda de Arango of Havana declared her wish that at her death her slaves María de los Angeles, María Catalina, Teresa, Nepomuceno, Fermín, and José María be set free of all captivity and servitude. Additionally, she ordered that Fermín be given 200 pesos in silver and her "set of kitchen utensils in remuneration for his good services." "For the same reason," she went on, "Nepomuceno should also get 200 pesos and for the special affection I have for them María de los Angeles, María Catalina, and Teresa should be given all the utensils to make pastries, [and] the small house I have in Santo Cristo, the three of them enjoying the usufruct of it, but belonging only to María de los Angeles and María Catalina, furthermore the three of them should receive 200 pesos." In addition, three other slaves received gifts: "the *morena* Clara will receive 350 pesos, Dolores 200, and Francisco another 200."[33]

There are instances when the instructions in a woman's will sound as if the executor was writing down her words verbatim, as she spoke. The result is a rambling, slightly ungrammatical document that gives the impression that sometimes only a comma or a colon separated a slave from his or her freedom. That is the case with María del Carmen Sotolengo Alfaro's last wishes. She was in a perfect position to exert her power when writing her will in 1871, as the Ten Years' War raged. She was wealthy, single, and without successors. She appointed her sister-in-law her universal heir but left many instructions when it came to her slaves. "It is my will," she declared, "that my slaves, ten-year-old María de las Mercedes, the daughter of María de los Angeles, already deceased, and María Jesús, Ursula's daughter, Juliana, four years old, daughter of said Ursula, who will also be set free, Bonifacio, approximately forty years old, his son Agustín, four years old, Manuel, twenty four years old more or less, José Coleto, fifty years old, Juan, eighteen years old, who will be free four years after my death, equally Norberto, twenty-eight years old, who will be freed after four years, same thing Vidal and Jorge Cayetano and Víctor Guadalupe and Andrea also free after four years." She then bequeathed the *liberta morena* (free Black woman) Josefa Sotolengo (probably her former slave, as she carried the same last name as the mistress) and the *parda* (mixed-race woman) María de las Mercedes, whom she set free, the right to live in or rent the annex to her house. But if her heirs wanted to use that space, then the freed women should be given 1,000 pesos, in other words, 500 pesos each, so that they could live with that credit; if one of them died, the other one should receive the corresponding part.[34]

The countess of Jaruco distributed her money, real estate, jewelry, and slaves among her relatives, thousands of pesos to be received by nephews and nieces, brother, and sister-in-law. For instance, her nephew, Mariano Arango, inherited 300 pesos, her slave Juan Bautista, and one of her pieces of jewelry or furniture, of his choice (*el que más le acomode*). Another nephew, Francisco Arango, as a show of the affection the countess always had for him and to reward him for all his attentions, was bequeathed a plantation with everything it contained, but with the condition that all the slaves there had to be *coartados* (with their price set at 300 pesos each) and that her servant Ignacio was to be set entirely free. Demonstrating the direct connection between loyalty to a mistress and the possibility of freedom, the countess wrote in her will that her slave Benedicto be given his freedom letter because of how faithful and affectionate a servant he had been, and she left him a house on Francisco de Paula Street. She asked her nephew, the marquis of Cárdenas, to keep Benedicto always under his protection, all these favors being deserved because of his "rare loyalty." The countess also left to a former slave (*mi liberto*, as she put it), the free Black man Felipe Santa Cruz (who had the same last name as hers), the house on O'Reilly Street where he was living at the time, and which she had purchased for him. Additionally, the same *liberto* was to receive six pieces of silver cutlery as well as a slave woman with her two children and two other slaves, one of them Creole. In that manner, the countess transformed her former slave into a slaveholder. She also left María Jesús, Felipe's daughter, a house located in the Calzada of San Luis Gonzaga. The countess charged her nephew, the marquis of Cárdenas, to intervene when necessary if he saw that slaves were being mistreated. Additionally, the countess's slave, the *morena criolla* (a Black woman born in Cuba) María de Loreto, received in usufruct a pent roof on Compostela Street, her manumission letter, and a slave, the *negra* Concepción—once again, transforming a loyal slave into a slaveholder overnight.

Francisca, a *negra criolla* (a Black woman born in Cuba), was less fortunate. The countess magnanimously agreed to set her *coartación* at 400 pesos even though the original price had been more than that. She confirmed the donations she had made to her former slave María Regla, whom she had freed when the slave married, including a house on San Francisco de Paula Street, two slaves—Antonia María and Francisco Antonio—and a plot in San Luis Gonzaga, "all of which she has already received." Clearly the countess's astonishing generosity with some of her slaves was based on her personal connections with those specific slaves, though her concern never made her question the institution of slavery. For example, she bequeathed to a relative, doña Josefa González, the *negrito* Antonio, Soledad's son; also Mateo, Gracia's son; and the *negrita* Francisca, or the Creole Teresa, whomever she fancied the most, as she put it. She left in captivity most of the hundreds of enslaved men, women, and children under her rule. Most of her assets—money, sugar mills, wrought silver, jewelry, furniture, and slaves—she left to her niece and universal heir.[35] That arbitrariness, the testaments shifting from one sentence to another between generous concern, which seemed to indicate that they viewed their slaves as individuals with personal needs, and cruel detachment that reflected their understanding of slaves as nothing but objects to be given to whomever they chose, is characteristic of nineteenth-century Cuban women's wills.

As mentioned, it was usually domestic slaves, because of their greater opportunity for personal interaction, who benefited the most from their mistresses' wills, but that was not always the case. Lucía Dunand, a French widow from Santiago who died in 1860, was the owner of several coffee plantations, other pieces of land, and fifty-four slaves. She bequeathed all her property, including the enslaved men and women under her authority, in equal parts to her nephew and granddaughter. But she made an exception with two slaves, both of them living on her *cafetal*. Prudencio Casamayor, her executor and himself one of the wealthiest men in eastern Cuba, faithfully recorded that "doña Lucía had already set free the *negras* Modesta and María from the *dotación* of the coffee plantation, for their good services, and having been asked specifically as her executor to give them their freedom without charging them anything, and her heirs having been aware of this decision, it is convenient to do so and I will verify it as soon as Your Excellency gives me permission to do it."[36] Magdalena Petit, from Santiago, died without succession, and she also decided to reward a number of both domestic and plantation slaves: "It is my will to bequeath, as I in fact bequeathed their freedom to my servants Justo, Creole, my coachman, Nicolás, also Creole, slave driver [*contramayoral*], Antoinette from Africa, and a field slave, all of whom I grant their manumission letter because of their good services. Equally, I bequeath in favor of the *morena* Caridad, creole, about forty-six years of age, who despite having been granted her freedom has stayed by my side, always providing me with the best care, the amount of 4,000 pesos that my executor will give her after my death."[37]

While some mistresses took the opportunity of writing their wills to display their gratitude to specific servants, others took a more detached approach: In 1829, María Ignacia de Contreras of Havana, widow of the marquis of San Felipe y Santiago, ordered that at her death "all the slaves of her plantations be given an extra set of clothing." She did not free any of her slaves; instead, she gave one of her slaves, *el negro* Juan *cocinero* (cook), to her oldest son; her personal servant, *el negro* Fernando, to don Pedro Cárdenas; and *el negro* Esteban and a maidservant to don Manuel O'Reilly, the count of Buenavista. She also left to don Joaquín de Santa Clara, the son of the count of Mopox, a slave from one of her plantations to be selected by her executors.[38]

It was not unusual for slaves, especially in rural areas, to run away for days or weeks, until hunger made them come back. Those short-term flights, Stephanie Camp reminds us while referring to the American South, were one of the many forms of resistance the enslaved population adopted in a daily tug-of-war to challenge the power of the master class.[39] Aware of that, the countess of Casa Montalvo in 1840 left instructions that at her death each of her slaves should receive 8 reales (silver coins), except for the ones who were "fugitives at that moment."[40]

There were times when mistresses' wills hung over slaves as a sword of Damocles, and forced them to be obedient and submissive in order to gain that elusive freedom. In 1803, for example, the countess of Jaruco stated that she wanted three of her slaves—a woman named María and two sisters, Francisca and Catalina—to be *coartadas* in the amount of 200 pesos each, so that they could not be sold for a higher price; it was "well understood," she stated, "that I grant them this kindness [*gracia*] if they continue to serve me well till I die." The slaves must have behaved satisfactorily, because a year later she added the following clause to her will: "In consideration of how deserving my slaves María, Francisca, and Catalina have been, I order the first one to be *coartada* at 100 pesos and the other two at 150 so that they cannot be sold for a higher amount when I die because it is my will [*por ser mi voluntad*]."[41]

As we have seen, most slaveholders who wanted to be generous and to free their slaves waited to do so until their death, creating chronic uncertainty for the men and women who hoped to receive their letter of manumission, and who, if they did, then had to deal with the question of whether or not the executors and heirs were willing to respect their mistresses' wills. Some slaveholding women were aware of the vulnerable position their slaves would find themselves in and reiterated their desire that their final wishes be respected. In 1846, Isabel Gomée, who owned a female slave named Micaela and her three children, Felicita, José, and Dionisio, stated in her testament: "It is my will that the said *negra* Micaela and her son Dionisio, a nursing baby, be free from the day I die in remuneration for her distinguished services and the constant assistance and love she has professed for me throughout all my sicknesses, this will should serve as their document to that end, and I request my heirs not to alter this manumission in any form, as I want them to let me enjoy the fulfillment of the favor I am granting." The will did not free the other two children of the loyal slave.[42]

In 1859, Manuela Pérez of Havana stated in her will that her slave, a fifteen-year-old mixed-race boy, be set free, and that her children should abide by her decision. "Being my last will," she declared in front of three male witnesses, "to set free my slave the mulatto Fernando Pérez who was born in my power, whom I raised, and for whom I have always had great consideration, and having promised to set him free at my death, I want no obstacle set to what I said to the referred mulatto, who is on this date fifteen or sixteen years old, and therefore I want my children to fulfill my wish."[43]

Not only was it unclear how faithfully executors and relatives would follow the instructions given in wills, but it was also uncertain how soon after writing their wills, in which slaves' manumission and other advantages were contemplated, slaveholding women would die. Leví Marrero mentions how, in a will signed in 1772, the count of Jaruco set free a young slave, *el negrito*

Felipe, but ordered that he should continue serving the countess and obtain his freedom only after her death.[44] The countess survived her husband by thirty-two years, but fortunately for the slave, she decided to free him (the date is unclear) before she died. That slave was the same Felipe whom the countess favored with a house and two slaves. In 1852, Josefa Reyna, who only owned one slave, left him free in her will, but with a set of conditions. Her testament reflects how married women found a way to wield power despite what the laws stated. Reyna thought of the young slave she owned as her property and thus considered herself, and not her husband, entitled to determine his future, at least up to a point: "It is my wish that if at the time of my death I have no legitimate successors, the *negrito* Serafio be freed of all subjection and captivity, granting this favor when he turns twenty-five years old or, if my husband dies earlier, in that case my . . . executor would give him the manumission letter." She lived for another thirty years, by which time "her *negrito*" was a grown man.[45]

While the deaths of mistresses could be good news for slaves, those deaths could also result in the separation of loved ones. Bárbara María Pérez of Santiago de Cuba was the owner of two slaves, a mother and daughter named Juana de Dios and Margarita, respectively. She left the mother to one of her own daughters and the enslaved child to her other daughter.[46] Josefa Ramírez y Morilla, a married woman who also had two female slaves, left one of them, Cándida, identified as Creole, to her daughter, and the other one, María Belén, to her husband with the condition that the enslaved woman should become free when he died.[47] When a Havana couple, Irino Linares and Margarita Ramos, wrote their will in 1866, they chose to distribute their slaves among their children. Their son Pedro was bequeathed the slaves Antonio, fifty years old; Encarnación, twelve; and Lázaro, twenty-one. Their daughter Victoria inherited Basilio, twenty-five years old; Eusebia, fourteen; and Rosario, fifty, who was left *coartada* (with her price set at 204 pesos). Their daughter Eleuteria inherited José, a nine-year-old boy; Merced, thirty years old; and Merced's three-year-old twins, Esteban and Juana. And their daughter Angelita was to get María, twenty-five; Petrona, forty; and Arcadia, twenty-three, and her three-year-old son José. Though they kept together the small children and their mothers, when examining the various lots, it seems that slaveholders were more concerned with equally bequeathing valuable slaves to their heirs than with keeping their slaves' family ties intact.[48]

Most people appointed friends or lawyers as executors, but it was also common to appoint one's spouse. In 1833, Josefa Antonia González's husband appointed her as one of two executors for their eight young children. In that capacity, after he died, she had to oversee the appraisal of the couple's properties, which included some of the following prices for their slaves:

the *negro de nación* (Black man born in Africa) Andrés, who was a maker of women's shoes, and thus a skilled worker, was valued at 450 pesos. Twenty-two-year-old Tomás, an apprentice shoemaker, was valued at only 300 pesos for health reasons (*por estar algo afectado de pecho*). The mixed-race Creole woman Pilar, forty-two years old and with all sorts of domestic skills (*general en todo servicio*), was valued at 600 pesos. Twenty-six-year-old Isabel, *negra de nación*, without a particular skill (*sin habilidad particular*), was valued at 350 pesos, and her six-month-old son Domingo at 50. The total value of the family's nine slaves was set at 2,800 pesos.[49] Antonio Romero, husband of Bárbara María Pérez, appointed his wife and eldest daughter María Francisca for "their integrity and good management" as his executors and granted the two of them "all power and faculties" required to distribute his assets among his large family, which included five sons and two daughters.[50]

Though not common, there were cases in which mistresses became so close to some young slaves, especially if they had acted as godmother to them, that they turned them into surrogate children.[51] Elena Ducté (also spelled Doute), a slaveholder from Santiago de Cuba who had been born in the French colony of Saint Domingue, formally adopted a slave girl and left her an inheritance. Ducté is never identified in her will as *doña*, but rather is given the title of *mademoiselle*. In the presence of two translators, she stated in her will that she herself was an illegitimate daughter and had remained single all her life, and was therefore without legitimate heirs—though, she revealed surprisingly, she herself had had seven illegitimate children, all of whom had died without successors (figure 4.1). When she wrote her will, she owned a small but debt-free house and corresponding plot on Gallo Street in Santiago, as well as eight slaves: Pedro, alias Primero; Sebastián, alias Luben; Sefiro; Esteban, alias Azoz; Antonia; Victoria; Isabel, alias Emé; and Noberta. Not having successors, she was free to leave her belongings to whomever she chose, presumably friends from the French community. She left Leonardo Vizet 200 pesos and appointed him her only and universal heir (*para que todo lo haya, goce y herede con la bendición de Dios en mi nombre*). She left three of the enslaved men—Pedro, Sebastián, and Sefiro—to don Antonio Vizet. She chose to set free the other five slaves—Esteban, Antonia, Victoria, and Isabel and her daughter Noberta—so that "they enjoy full freedom after my days, getting the corresponding manumission letters." What made her free five of her slaves and keep three of them in bondage? As seen previously, the reasons why some slaves were freed and others were not seemed to depend on personal ties with their mistresses. Slaves who had the opportunity to be perceived as loyal, faithful, affectionate, and useful, those who were in contact with their owners regularly enough to form personal ties, were the

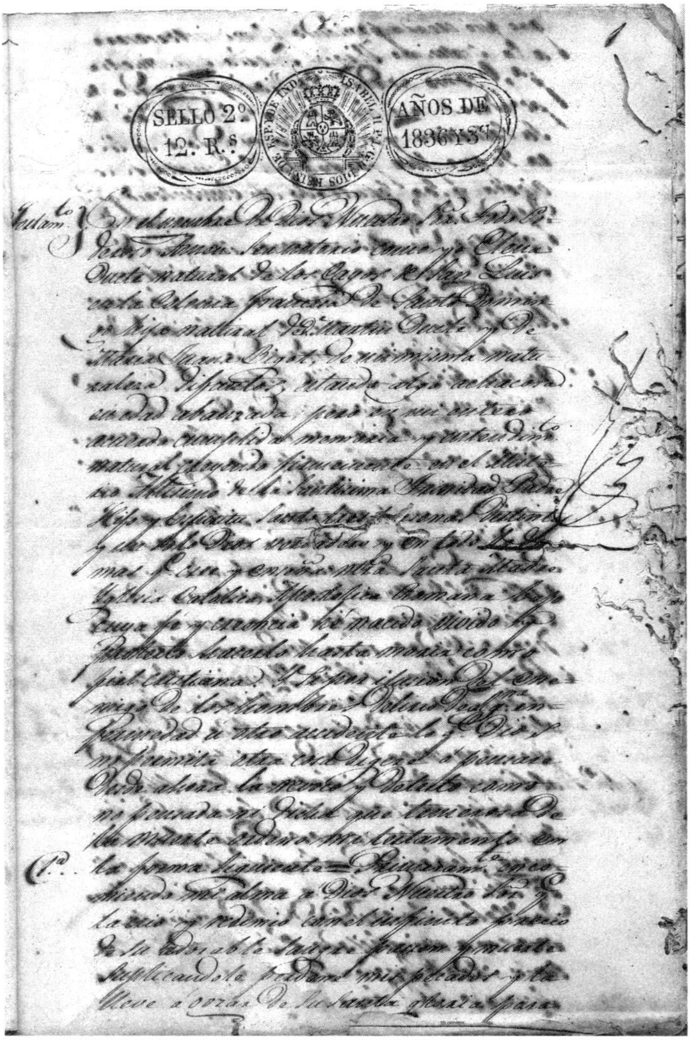
SELLO 2º
12. R.s
AÑOS DE
1836 Y 37

Figure 4.1. Elena Ducté's will. ANRC, Audiencia de Santiago de Cuba, leg. 63, no. 1573.

ones most likely to be set free or to receive other testimonies of appreciation. Ducté's testament includes a document confirming the executor's issuance of the manumission letters to the slaves who were to be freed.

The most interesting aspect of this will, however, is Elena Ducté's relationship with a slave girl who became her goddaughter. Ducté's will includes an 1828 baptism certificate of a girl described as the illegitimate child of a slave, Isabel; Isabel was owned by Gustavo Bessé, a friend of Ducté. The priest performed "solemn baptism" and stated that the girl was set free after being baptized. Bessé and Ducté acted as the child's godparents, the priest reminding them that by doing so they had assumed a spiritual relationship and important obligations. The girl was named Elena Ducté, like her godmother, and two years before dying, the older woman included the child in her will, leaving her 200 pesos. By the time the mistress died, in 1840, the girl was only twelve years old, thus requiring the selection of a tutor, a task that was undertaken with great seriousness by all involved, as indicated by the records. After consultation, the executors appointed don Próspero Chaillon, who accepted and swore to faithfully fulfill his job of caring for, educating, and teaching his charge, as well as providing nourishment and other needs with the interest gained from the 200 pesos that her godmother Elena Ducté had left her. He signed a document promising to defend the child, and to make sure to preserve the legacy and other goods that belonged to her, so that she would receive the intact amount with the interest.[52]

After women made their wills, all that was left to do was to sign them, a task some of them could not perform because they were illiterate. (As we have seen earlier, according to the 1862 Census, nearly two-thirds of the white female population could not read or write.) María Caridad Méndez's testament ends with the formula: "consents and doesn't sign because she said she does not know how, at her request one of her witnesses signed for her [*otorga y no firma porque dijo no saber, lo hace a su ruego uno de los testigos*]."[53] In 1859 Manuela Pérez stated that "not knowing how to sign, don Felipe de la Cruz and other witnesses, all of them residents of Havana, signed in her place."[54] In contrast, as early as 1789, Inés González de Carbajal was able to sign her own will with the usual formula, "and thus I declare and sign [*y así lo declaro y firmo*]."[55]

For many nineteenth-century Cuban women, their testaments were the only opportunity they had to leave a record of who they were, even when they were illiterate, as they dictated their last wishes to their executor. Wills allow us to hear, if weakly, a trace of the woman's personal voice. And yet the documents are elusive, frustrating even, in how much they fail to reveal. Consider the testament of Angela Casamayor, a woman from Santiago de Cuba. The will she made in 1853 provides considerable information about her life: she stated that she had been a slave under Prudencio Casamayor, who happened to be one of Cuba's wealthiest men in the early 1800s. A native of Saint Domingue, like many slaveholders, Casamayor had dragged his slaves to eastern Cuba to escape Haiti's revolution.[56] At some uncertain date, he granted Angela her freedom and made her, as she put it, "an emancipated slave from the house of Prudencio Casamayor Sr. [*una liberta de la casa de Prudencio Casamayor, padre*]." In her will, she declared that she was the illegitimate daughter of a woman named Susana, whose last name she could not remember, having arrived in Santiago when she was an infant. Never married and with no descendants, she was, in her estimation, approximately sixty-six years old at the time of making her will. Her estate, which she shared with a *pardo* (mixed-race man) named Guillermo Panten, included seven slaves: two *negras* named María and Margarita, a *mulatica* (little mulatta) named Petrona, and four *negritos* named Susana, Andrés, Manuel, and Victorina. She left *el quinto líquido* (the fifth of her estate) to *la parda* Carlota Panten, possibly Guillermo's daughter, as proof of the special affection she had for her, "having taken care of her since childhood [*de haberla manoseado desde su infancia*]." The rest of the estate went to her "partner" Guillermo Panten, who was appointed her only and universal heir, "so that he could enjoy her legacy with God's blessing and in her name." The testament ends with the common formula: "no signature because she doesn't know how to sign [*no firma porque no sabe*]."[57] In other words, despite being illiterate, through her own words, recorded as faithfully as possible by the executor, Angela Casamayor let us know what her approximate birthdate was, her birthplace, her mother's name, and who her family's master had been. We learn that she was a slaveholder and that she was able to carve a space in society secure enough to become financially independent as a small property owner. She was able to establish family ties with her partner and his daughter, and she was prosperous and autonomous enough to leave an inheritance to a man she was not married to. However, her will remains silent about many important facets of her life. We learn nothing about when and how she came to be free, and how she, a former slave, felt about owning seven slaves. Wills, constricted as they were by a formulaic and legal language, are not a fully satisfying reflection of a life's experience, but in many cases, as in the case of Angela Casamayor, a testament is all we have to conjure a woman's past and her role as a slaveholder.

CONCLUSION

Inhabiting a society where they had a subordinate civil and political status, and little access to education, nineteenth-century Cuban women often took the opportunity to state in their wills, even when the women were illiterate, what they wanted the nature of their legacy to be. Not only single women and widows but also married women, no matter what the law said, assumed the right to determine the fate of those they considered their property. Women's wills reveal a wide spectrum of attitudes on the part of female slaveholders toward their slaves that ranged from cold detachment to warm personal connection. The documents reflect how women exercised the power they had to reward or punish a slave, by providing them a chance for freedom or by failing to do so. Furthermore, when slaveholders distributed their slaves among friends and relatives as gifts, that could greatly affect those slaves' lives. Wills, formulaic and incomplete documents as they are, expand our understanding of women's lives, their material world, and their roles as slaveholders.

5

Amas and the Ten Years' War

Camaguey and surrounding areas, west of Oriente, was where most of the fighting against Spain took place during the first serious challenge to the colonial status quo, the devastating Ten Years' War (1868–78). Examining slaveholding women's involvement in the Ten Years' War helps us understand more clearly how owning domestic slaves impacted the economic lives of white women, and how gender relations intruded upon the rebels' views on the institution of slavery. The military conflict tested the limits of these women's incipient abolitionist positions.

In 1868, Cuba's eastern provinces rose against the Spanish colonial government. Lack of political representation, along with heavy taxes, debt, and financial constraints to trade with the United States and other markets, led small plantation owners, cattle ranchers, and entrepreneurs to rebel against what they believed was a corrupt and unfair regime. In the western and central provinces, the island's slaveholding elite, the powerful sugar plantation owners, who were continuing to benefit from the expansion of the sugar economy, relied on the Spanish army to ensure that their large numbers of slaves remained in bondage. However, the leaders of the Ten Years' War, who tended to own fewer slaves, were less fearful of slave rebellions. Slavery for them was a source of wealth, but not the most important one. Spain's protectionist policies, its opposition to free trade, limited the economic freedoms that this area's businessmen required to thrive, while also subjecting them to a subordinate political position. Their identity as modern, cultured Creole entrepreneurs made them highly critical of the colonial system, and led them to support, if hesitantly, the gradual abolition of slavery, a position that gave Black freedpeople a reason to join the insurrection. In Oriente, Las Villas, and particularly in Camaguey, thousands of families were drawn into the conflict as men and women sided with the rebellion. In Puerto Príncipe, Camaguey's main town and the center of the insurgency, as well as in other

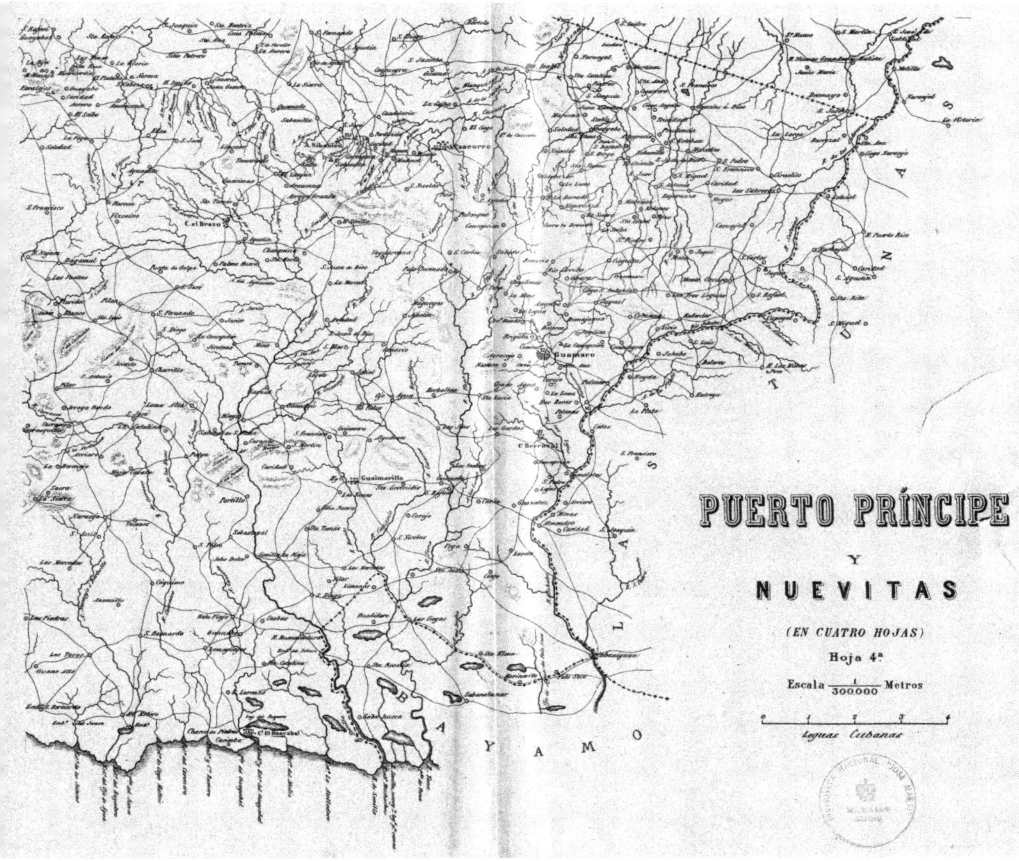

Figure 5.1. Map of Puerto Príncipe and Nuevitas. From Antonio Pirala, *Anales de la Guerra de Cuba* (Madrid: Felipe Fernández Rojas, 1895).

localities, colonial authorities stepped up their vigilance with regard to potential suspects, closed publications that were critical of the government, and suspended cultural activities that town dwellers could use to promote their views (figure 5.1). As the political climate deteriorated, property owners, cattle ranchers, sugar planters, and businessmen, many of them members of the region's elite, abandoned their comfortable houses and fled to the nearby hills and mountains to join the rebel army. Some rebels brought their families and slaves along, others left them behind.

Determined to put an end to the war, the Spanish government set out to punish the rebels in every possible way, even if many of the men, as soldiers of the Cuban republican army, were out of reach. Cubans accused of being disloyal to Spain were labeled *infidentes*, a broad term that included, among other offenses, treason, rebellion, insurrection, conspiracy, sedition, support to rebels and criminals, and sharing of information with the enemy. These were crimes punishable with jail, deportation, and death.[1]

The outbreak of the Ten Years' War coincided with Spain's political upheaval known as the Gloriosa Revolution, in which a liberal political class, many of whom had family and economic ties to the Cuban planter class, dethroned Queen Isabel II. The 1868 military coup was led by Juan Prim, who sought to turn Spain into a constitutional monarchy. The liberal class endorsed an economic policy that benefited the sugar elite by favoring free trade with the United States, much to the consternation of the Spanish financial and commercial oligarchy in Cuba, whose members defended protectionist policies.[2] The most reactionary loyalists took advantage of Spanish liberalism's uncertain future, organizing, independently of Madrid, to defend the interests of the peninsular elite and punish the rebellion with volunteer militias. They succeeded at adding the confiscation of property to the penalties enemies of Spain could suffer. Using the rationale that the insurrection favored the abolition of slavery and therefore was willing to deprive slaveholders of an important source of income, colonial authorities proceeded to take control of the rebels' wealth, including their slaves.[3] Reform-minded Domingo Dulce, appointed captain general, Cuba's highest authority, by the Gloriosa and with family ties to the sugar planter class, lasted only six months in his position, and even before leaving, he had given in to the intransigent *peninsulares*. Following a more conservative turn of the Spanish administration, it was Dulce who issued, and his more conservative successor Antonio Caballero de Rodas who reaffirmed, the suspension of civil rights on the island and an embargo policy that would shatter the economic foundation of the eastern provinces.[4]

The colonial government created a *consejo administrativo* (administrative council) to regulate how the confiscated property was to be handled, but the process was extremely chaotic. Local and government authorities interpreted the law in different ways, neighbors used this opportunity to solve personal vendettas, and corrupt officials exploited it for their personal gain. The confiscated goods could be given to one individual who had earned the authorities' trust or divided up among several residents, the authorities being mindful of how to distribute those goods in a way that was most beneficial for the state coffers. If the rebel whose property was confiscated had debts, the law stated that an effort should be made to benefit the lender, but only if the lender was loyal to Spain.

Ann Stoler, prompted by her study of the Dutch state's role in Indonesia, has characterized the colonial archive as reflecting an empire's futile attempt to create the illusion that "all was in order, because papers classified people, because directives were properly acknowledged, and because colonial civil servants were schooled to assure that papers were prepared, circulated, securely stored, and sometimes rendered to ash."[5] The anxiety and uncertainty Stoler identified in the Dutch bureaucracy can also be found in colonial Cuba, with various levels of state and local authorities contradicting each other, dragging things out through orders and counterorders, arguments and counterarguments, that went back and forth between the localities' *inspectores de vigilancia*, the men in charge of confiscating the property; the *tenientes gobernadores*, the heads of each political jurisdiction who issued the orders; authorities in Havana; and those in Madrid, who intervened when there were appeals. "We can't forget," Moreno Fraginals wrote, "that traditional history is written with papers."[6] Bureaucrats were hard at work leaving traces of an official past, and though the history they recorded is fragmented, with their legal documents filed on two sides of the Atlantic, and stored in multiple archives, certain facts are clear. Within a year, thousands of houses, along with furniture and personal items, libraries, small and large plantations, fruit farms, cattle, horses, poultry, tools, sugar, tobacco, and businesses, as well as bank accounts, stocks, and other sources of wealth, had been confiscated from people labeled *infidentes*. The loss of property reached nearly 20 million pesos, an amount that grew throughout the war. This first round of embargos also included about five thousand slaves, who had been under the power of owners who were now considered disloyal.[7] During the investigation, local authorities recruited neighbors to inform on neighbors and to help them procure lists of the enslaved men, women, and children the insurgents counted among their possessions.

The National Archive in Madrid houses hundreds of petitions sent by Cuban women whose property had been confiscated, requesting the return of their assets, particularly their slaves, with the corresponding, though at times inconclusive, governmental response. Depending on the women's or their relatives' involvement in subversive activities, the authorities could accept, deny their request, or find a compromise by withdrawing some of their belongings and releasing others. As usual, those with power dominate the archives. It was mostly women of comfortable means, who had suffered great losses, including their slaves, and whose social standing had plummeted, who dared to file a complaint challenging the government's decision. Many other women who were also penalized for their political views did not have the wherewithal to protest and had few assets to recover.

Historians have wrestled with trying to understand the insurrection's views on the subject of slavery, especially in the early period, and have pointed out that it is difficult to reach a general conclusion because there was no consensus among the rebels—their positions were conflicted and ever evolving. Mocking the contradictions of the "modern" Cuban man, the poet Enrique José Varona wrote that "he has read Proudhon, goes everywhere by carriage, loves freedom and owns slaves."[8] Although the eastern provinces were not as dependent on slave labor as other parts of the island, that did not mean that those who owned slaves were eager to give them up. While many property owners understood that supporting slavery would have placed them on the same side as a government they opposed, their slaves were still a crucial investment. Despite their ambivalence, in 1869 the rebel forces at their Constitutional Assembly in Guáimaro, Camaguey, declared the abolition of slavery in the territory they controlled, thus positioning the insurgency as a modern, principled alternative to a retrograde colonial power. Article 24 of the Guáimaro Constitution, voted by representatives of the three main areas that had risen against the colonial power (Oriente, Las Villas, and Camaguey), declared: "All inhabitants of the Republic are entirely free."[9] The process of freeing the enslaved population was anything but smooth, as many slaveholders were reluctant to part with a labor force they had relied on for generations. "Opposing slavery," writes David Sartorius, "did not overlap neatly with opposing empire."[10] Ultimately, however, the insurgents realized that maintaining slavery was not compatible with their vision of a "free Cuba." They also understood the price they would pay: their commitment to abolition irreparably damaged their ties with plantation owners in western and central Cuba, and destroyed any hope they had that this wealthy segment would support the insurrection.

The voluminous collection of petitions to colonial authorities from individuals attempting to recover their slaves reveals that slavery, while attacked on the insurgents' political platforms, continued to be defended and embraced by many insurgents, especially by those women for whom enslaved labor was their only financial source of income. Women, even those critical of the colonial government, filed request upon request to get their confiscated property back, including their houses and personal possessions. In 1870, Justina Denoyé, like many other women of comfortable means, wrote to the colonial authorities asking for the devolution of her furniture, which she carefully listed: two wardrobes, two beds, a dressing-table, a dresser, a wash-stand, a piano, more than a dozen chairs, two pairs of balances, a rug and chair for church, all the house linen, the family portraits, two basins, a lyre, a small lamp, two bedsteads, a mahogany crib, and a small mahogany paper basket.[11] But by and large, the women's most urgent petition was to have their slaves returned. Their agonizing statements reveal how crucial the work of their rented slaves was for the survival of slaveholders and their families, and how white women, insurgents or not, continued to think of owning slaves as their right. Even if many of these women had shared their fathers', husbands', and sons' commitment to the ideals of a "free Cuba," their inability to survive and feed their families on their own made them hold on to their condition as slaveholders.

When men went to fight and were identified as rebels, their property was confiscated. Their wives, sisters, or other female relatives found themselves as heads of the households, with children to feed and without the resources they were accustomed to. This situation could be permanent if the man died in battle, a common occurrence in a war that left thousands of soldiers dead—fathers, husbands, brothers, sons—making the women's lives even more precarious. What they counted on to help their families survive was slave labor. The economic significance of slavery becomes clear when examining the documents women sent to their local authorities. The petitioners used a variety of arguments to get their slaves back, including claims that their men folk were innocent, that the confiscated property belonged to them and not their husbands, or that as women they were not politically involved. The most common argument or strategy, however, was trying to appeal to the authorities' sympathy by referring to the life of poverty that had resulted from the confiscation of their property and the loss of their slaves. And this was not an overstatement. They did depend on their slaves' work to maintain their way of life. In 1852, in a letter to a church official in Puerto Príncipe, the archbishop of Santiago de Cuba, Antonio María Claret, observed that white people in Cuba did not like to work, and white Creoles even less, especially the women: "Ladies never work," he wrote, "poor women, do a bit of sewing, it is Black women who do everything, they wash, they iron."[12] There were few large sugar or coffee plantations in Camaguey and therefore no need for one person to own numerous slaves. Domestic slavery, however, was a different story. In Puerto Príncipe and other towns in the region, domestic slaves were common, many of them working in the household, and many of them hired out and supplying their owners an income with their wages. Cuban historian Elda Cento Gómez has observed that rented-out slaves provided white families with financial stability, and that they were often bought with that purpose in mind.[13] Because the slaves enjoyed a certain level of autonomy and were integrated into the household's life, white families, insurgent or not, tended to think of this type of enslavement as benign (as opposed to what went on at a plantation). That attitude, and their financial exigency, perhaps helped the women reconcile their anticolonial views, when they had them, with their insistence on recovering their slaves.

In 1871 in Puerto Príncipe, Asunción Estrada wrote to the authorities after being accused of disloyalty and of helping the insurrection. The daughter of wealthy parents, she had lived a comfortable and leisurely life in the country.

She was the owner of several slaves whom she had rented out to people living in town and who helped provide for her, as a widow, and her two children. After someone claimed to have seen her sewing buttons and stitching clothes worn by the rebels, her slaves were confiscated. Estrada admitted to sewing clothes for the insurgents, but the clothes, she argued, were for family members, and she was therefore fulfilling her obligation as a woman. It was unfair, she reasoned, to charge a seamstress for her stitches. She sewed for her brother and brother-in-law out of affection for them. All she wanted was to recover her four slaves, Eleizo, Isidoro, Valentín, and Pablo, so she could rent them out again. In January 1873, two years after her initial request, the government agreed to return the enslaved men to her.[14]

On paper, the rebels' wives, heirs, and relatives were not affected by confiscations, unless they had also been accused of government disloyalty. However, considering women's subordinate legal status, when the government took over their fathers' or husbands' assets, the women's economic circumstances were immediately altered. In 1871, María de la Caridad Pérez y Salas, a resident of Sancti Spíritus, asked the authorities to have the property of her father, an insurgent who had died in the war, released to her. More specifically, she needed her father's three slaves—named María Magdalena, María de los Santos, and Esteban—because, as she explained, she was a widow, "absolutely destitute," and had no other resources. After confirming the death of her father, investigating her moral and political behavior, and finding that she had not helped the insurgency, the government complied.[15] María Guerra, an *infidente* from Puerto Príncipe who had been left to provide for her grandchildren after her son was killed in the war, wrote a petition explaining that she was completely impoverished, and unable to find a job due to her advanced age. She asked the government to return some of her belongings, including two slaves: *el negro* Lino, who was part of her dowry, and *la negra* Felicita, who had belonged to her deceased son. The government agreed to let her keep a house and the slave Lino, but nothing else.[16]

The women's complaints about their miserable living conditions were not an exaggeration. In addition to their vulnerable position as victims of the government embargo, they suffered the effects of the region's economic collapse during the military conflict. In the early years of the war, the insurrection succeeded in taking control of the rural areas. In Puerto Príncipe, the center of the insurrection, the rebel army cut off regular communications between town and country, and disrupted the arrival of food. Markets and stores stopped selling vegetables, meat, milk, and bread. Hunger became widespread, and the dependence on hired slaves more desperate. Throughout the eastern provinces, families who had previously enjoyed a comfortable economic situation now found themselves destitute. A widow named

Cupertina de la Cruz filed a petition to get back the confiscated property of her dead husband, including furniture, clothes, and several slaves. She acknowledged that she had already been allowed to recover two slaves, Federico and María, as well as a few pieces of furniture, but she herself lived in complete poverty, she stated, and had four children to feed. The earnings of the two slaves were insufficient to support the family, especially because there were times when the slaves failed to find a place to work. She requested a house to live in and a few more slaves, so that with the product of their work she could clothe and feed her family, and attend to their needs.[17] Another widow, Juana Sánchez, claimed that she and her family were living in a state of extreme poverty, and asked the government to let her keep her six slaves, two men and four women. The money the rented slaves earned, she wrote, supported her and her whole family, consisting of twelve members, while also supplying the rented slaves' needs. The government agreed to let her have the slaves.[18] Representing a minor in 1871, a lawyer from Puerto Príncipe contacted the authorities in defense of Irene Suaces, the orphaned daughter of a wealthy man whose rural properties, a sugar mill and a cattle ranch, had been destroyed as punishment for his role in the insurgency. Of the 131 slaves the family had owned before the war, only 21 remained, the rest having been confiscated. The situation, the attorney argued, was "unsustainable" for the girl and her older siblings, all of whom were blameless and had never done anything to displease the government. The petition requested the distribution of those twenty-one slaves among the heirs.[19] The outcome of the case is unknown.

A widow, Cristina Ramírez, requested that the government confirm her ownership of a fourteen-year-old pregnant girl named Caridad, who had belonged to her husband, an insurgent, because the family, including her four small children, had no other property to help them survive. Though not mentioned, the probable fate of the fourteen-year-old pregnant girl was to be hired out as a wet nurse, her wages contributing in a significant manner to the family's budget. Marissa Fuentes has observed that in slave societies, "enslaved women's sexual and reproductive capacities were used to further the wealth and status of . . . white women. Consequent to this dynamic of profit, images of enslaved women as sexually available and white women as virtuous persisted throughout the century."[20] Those contrasting images were deeply embedded in nineteenth-century Cuban culture as well, and helped rationalize the young female slaves' exploitation. Six months after Cristina Ramírez's request, the government agreed to let the widow keep the fourteen-year-old slave, Caridad.[21]

A woman named Rosa Morales Salazar also requested the release of a confiscated slave child, the twelve-year-old Eduardo Isabel, who had been in her property since he was born, as proved by the baptism certificate she included. Though the petition did not mention how Salazar planned to profit from the slave child, the arguments she used to convince the authorities—that she herself was an orphan, and that he was "all she owned"—seem to suggest that the reason she wanted the child back had less to do with affection and more with financial calculation, their long connection notwithstanding.[22] Even an enslaved child could be a significant source of income. Agueda Rodríguez, writing from Havana, asked that her daughter, the wife of an insurgent who had escaped to Yucatán, be given back her properties, including the rent of a house she owned and a young slave named Damián, as the only resources she had to feed her four small children.[23] In contrast, a woman named Leonor Schwerer claimed to be motivated by personal and not financial reasons when she asked the authorities to give her back two slaves belonging to her husband, who was accused of being an insurrectionist. She wanted to keep sixty-year-old Lucas, who was blind and crippled, and ten-year-old Manuel, despite their unprofitability, for the affection she had for them and for their good behavior. The authorities granted her request.[24]

Inspired by the rebels' promise of abolishing slavery and taking advantage of the chaotic social fluidity the war brought, thousands of slaves also joined the insurrection, either with their owners' blessings or against their will. In either case, mistresses had to survive now without the protection of their husbands and without the labor of their slaves. In 1868, a widow named Mariana de Quesada, whose husband had died on the battlefield, was forced to support their six young children with her personal work. Stating in her petition what tears she had shed, she asked the authorities to let her have access to the few goods the family had left, including their slaves. After a two-year investigation, the police concluded that of the four slaves the family had owned, only one, twenty-year-old Ireno, was in town and working for the widow. The others—Trina, who was thirty years old; Florencia, seven; and Juan Antonio, no age given—were assumed to have joined the insurrection. The government agreed to let her keep Ireno, given the widow's meager means and the fact that she herself was not accused of *infidencia*.[25]

In the case of married couples, it was usually the men and not the women who were accused of disloyalty to the government, prompting the wives to use the argument that the slaves should be returned because they were part of their dowries and thus belonged to them and not to their husbands. Officially, the confiscation policy did not extend to the wives' dowries. According to Spanish law, women lost control of their property when they married, but they, and not their husbands, remained the owners of the dowry, even if their husbands managed the assets. This was an important legal right that gave women a certain degree of financial independence. José Ramón Sánchez

Betancourt, an officer with the rebel army, complained in his memoirs that the official goal of the confiscation policy was to deprive those who fought against Spain of their resources, not to target the soldiers' relatives. And yet, he lamented, the appropriations extended to the paraphernalia and dowries of the rebels' wives, as well as their children's property.[26]

A petitioner named Angela Aguero y Guerra acknowledged that her husband had in fact left Puerto Príncipe for a while, not to fight, but simply to take care of his rural properties. He had then, she claimed, been forced to accept a temporary position with the insurgent government. He went back to his home and family as soon as he could, only to have the family's belongings (including hers) confiscated, even though she had not been accused of anything. The petitioner included with her request a *carta dotal* (dowry letter) to prove her point. We can only speculate about what prompted this couple to write the dowry letter in the first place—perhaps her wealthy parents' concern about their son-in-law's improper behavior. The document, signed in Puerto Príncipe in 1851, thirteen years after the couple were married, certified that the husband had received, from the assets his wife had inherited from her parents and grandparents, various properties valued at 12,000 pesos. By the terms of this document, if the marriage was dissolved, he agreed to return the dowry by paying 12,000 pesos to his wife, doña Angela Aguero, in cash, or by letting her select the best property he owned to compensate for the 12,000 pesos. Declaring that there had been no harm or deception, he renounced the laws that favored him, as the husband, and agreed not to subject his wife's dowry to his debt, crimes, or excesses. Both husband and wife were present at the signing, in addition to three witnesses, and both stated that they accepted the document willingly. Doña Angela signed with a cross. Twenty years later, in 1871, she sent the government a petition lamenting the miserable living conditions her once wealthy family, including four granddaughters, found itself in after all their belongings had been taken away. Even though they had been allowed to keep one slave, named Carlos, he was over fifty, with a wounded hand, and therefore not profitable, she argued. Doña Angela asked for the authorities' clemency and requested several more slaves whose labor could help feed the family. The authorities were not moved and declined to comply, arguing that the husband, a former rebel, was at home and that he could work and help support his relatives.[27]

A widow, Teresa Estrada y Pernas, also used the argument of her dowry in her request to get back her slave, named Crispina, and Crispina's young children, Pedro, Antonio, Gabriela, and José. Crispina's oldest child, Benjamín, and other slaves, all belonging to her deceased husband, Mariano Zayas, had been sent to Havana, but Crispina and her young children were the widow's exclusive property. In this case, what the mistress was seeking was not monetary profit but help with domestic chores. As she was a widow in poor health, without resources, and with ten children, it was urgent, she pleaded, to get back her slave and the four enslaved children. The slave woman would help her run the household with its numerous members. And the children would not be profitable in any way, she reassured the authorities, due to their youth.[28]

If living conditions for urban dwellers were dismal, the war also brought hardship to the rural areas. To prevent inhabitants of the countryside from supporting the insurgency, the government issued orders asking the rural population to turn themselves in to the nearby town's authorities. A woman named Mercedes de Aguero wrote a complaint stating that, following the government's instructions, she and her family had left the countryside and reported to the town's authorities. And yet, despite their obedience, their belongings had been taken away, with the exception of her slave Dolores and Dolores's child Agapito, both of them part of her dowry. She had also been allowed to keep, from the marriage assets, a slave named Genoveva and her children, Ramona and Rosa, who were nine and three years old. Dolores, however, had an injured foot and was therefore useless, and Genoveva, when rented out, earned 7 pesos, an amount that was not enough to cover the basic needs of the family, consisting of ten people. They found themselves barefoot, half-naked, and sick for lack of food. Their only hope was to get some additional slaves back. The government's response was to confirm the five slaves already granted and to deny any further release of property, with the same argument used in the cases already discussed: The husband was present, and he could find a job to support his family.[29]

Belén Abad de Aguero, married to an insurrectionist, declared that in February 1871, she and her family had left the countryside and reported to the town authorities as ordered. A month later, all their belongings had been taken from them, including the slave Ruperta with her daughter Caridad, as well as two other slaves, Cayetano and Antonia, who, when rented out, earned 16 pesos. That amount helped support twelve family members, all of whom, including the petitioner, were suffering from hunger, lack of clothing, and other kinds of deprivation that, she explained, she would not enumerate out of delicacy. A year later, the government confirmed she could keep temporary possession of those slaves.[30]

At times, a petition could backfire: only people who had been accused of insurrection could request to "borrow back" their slaves or own them temporarily. But each town and each set of local authorities handled the slippery legality in a different manner, thus creating myriad confusing circumstances and abuses. One woman, named Rafaela Hurtado, following the government's orders, had reported to the town's authorities on December 23, 1870, in the company of her whole family. In her petition she stated that, not having any means of subsistence, she had requested and received temporarily a confiscated female slave (who had belonged to an unspecified owner). The slave in question was a sixty-year-old woman named Mariana who worked for her but who, given her advanced age, could not be rented out to help support the four members of her family. Hurtado explained that all she could rely on were her own meager wages as a seamstress when she could find work. Before the war, she had owned a sewing machine, which was confiscated with her brother's properties. She asked the government to return either the sewing machine or its cost. The authorities' response was that, as an insurgent, her brother had had his property confiscated, including the sewing machine. She, however, was not accused of anything, and no property had been taken away from her; therefore, she had no right to the slave, who should be returned to the government.[31]

The insurgency achieved major victories in the early years of the war, but by 1870, as the Spanish army began to regain control of rebel territory, the Cuban fighters' situation became desperate, and so did the situation for the thousands of families who had joined the fighters in the *manigua* (uncultivated countryside). The war shattered the rebel family; it scattered its members, reduced them to poverty, and devastated its numbers; the living conditions were especially shocking for the most affluent ones, who had never before endured hardship.[32] A good example is the fate of Salvador Cisneros Betancourt's family. A wealthy landowner and a known critic of the colonial power, Cisneros Betancourt became a target of the colonial authorities as soon as the war began. Feeling threatened, the Cisneros Betancourt clan, one of the most respected in Puerto Príncipe, fled to the country in support of the insurrection. The government response was swift: all the family's property was confiscated, including their slaves. As was the case with many other rebel families, their experience in the *manigua* was tragic. They suffered hunger, sickness, and all sorts of challenges. After Cisneros Betancourt's wife and two of his daughters died, the remaining women and children were forced to turn themselves in.[33] It was a common predicament: men and women who had left their town residence to support the insurgents had to make a decision, either continue fighting or report to the Spanish authorities in Puerto Príncipe or other locations under the thumb of the colonial rulers.

The colonial authorities encouraged the rebels' *presentaciones* (capitulations), which, as Ada Ferrer has pointed out, allowed them to portray themselves as magnanimous figures willing to forgive their ill-behaved children.[34] Hungry, defeated, and humiliated, hundreds of the rebels filed daily back to their old homes, homes that were often no longer available to them because of the confiscations. Their years in the *manigua* had reduced their numbers, as their members had fallen victim to disease, starvation, and the battlefield. Once inside the towns, and lacking a regular source of income, they continued to face precarious and even desperate living conditions. This was the case for one Encarnación Varona, who belonged to an old Camagueyan family. Her attitude about her slaves reflects the group's ambivalence when it came to abolition. When her family left Puerto Príncipe to join the insurgency, she brought along her eleven children and her slave Dorotea, who remained in bondage and working for the family. Varona's mother-in-law also brought her slaves, one of whom would marry Dorotea in a civil ceremony while they all hid in the mountains. And when the circumstances became unbearably difficult and the Varona family decided to go back and report to the Spanish authorities, they took their slaves back with them, after warning them that by staying with their masters they would miss the opportunity to be free that the rebels were offering. Once in town, Encarnación Varona tried to rent out Dorotea to help the family survive. By then, however, the enslaved woman had a three- or fourth-month-old baby, the town was so poor that few people had money to hire her, and she often had to work just for food.[35] Many slaves stayed with masters who would not or could not provide even food. Were they counting on at least having a roof over their head? Was it a sense of loyalty, affection for their masters?

Elda Cento wonders why a slave like Dorotea did not run away. Why did she follow her mistress when the rebels were promising the abolition of slavery? Could it have been fear, gratitude, the feeling that the war had little to do with them? Could it have been the unbearable physical conditions faced in the *manigua*?[36] She herself suggests an answer when she describes the characteristics of the institution of slavery in Camaguey. Cento argues that in this region, where plantations or cattle ranches were small, and where domestic slaves were common, slaveholders knew all their slaves by name, had a closer interaction with them, and could more convincingly play the role of benevolent patriarch or matriarch. That personal relationship would have been significant when encouraging the slave population to follow them to the countryside and back to the towns, or urging them to fight by their side, and also when making promises of a future manumission.[37] That hope of bettering their personal circumstances as reward for their loyalty was also what the colonial government counted on, as David Sartorius has noted, to entice African-descended people to side with Spain during the Ten Years' War.[38]

Many women accused of *infidencia* suffered political repression and had their slaves confiscated, not because of their husbands' views, but because of their own. The Ten Years' War sharpened the distinctions between *peninsulares* and Cubans, colonizer and colonized. Men's and women's opposition to the political status quo helped create a sense of a new nation and culture, with its own traditions and views that were different from those of the colonial rulers. As Moreno Fraginals wrote, Creole women were a key factor in the formation of a Cuban identity.[39] Not surprisingly, they were also the target of repressive policies, including the confiscation of their slaves. After examining the files at Cuba's National Archive (ANRC) of individuals accused of disloyalty who were victims of confiscations, Cuban historian Doneya Gómez Véliz concluded that the women received the same treatment as the men, in terms of both the property lost and their sentences. She provides as example the legal case (*expediente gubernativo*) against Clementina Céspedes from Bayamo, accused of *infidencia*, in which every step for confiscating her property was rigorously followed. The authorities appropriated Felipa Céspedes, Clementina's twenty-year-old slave, described as Creole with matted hair and brown eyes, who worked at domestic chores, and another slave, María del Rosario Forraris, whom she owned with her husband. The document stipulated that no person was allowed to engage in any sort of commercial transaction with the *infidente* under penalty of law.[40] María Eugenia Latour is another example of a politically engaged woman, who was targeted by the government, and who persisted in her right to own slaves. She was a resident of Holguín, whose participation in war activities became known to the authorities. In 1872 she was condemned to a three-year jail sentence, the punishment later commuted to exile on the Isle of Pines. After serving her sentence, and therefore, she argued, being once again in full possession of her civil rights, she asked the authorities to return her confiscated slaves, named Constancia, Simona, José, Elías, and Margarita, as they were the only patrimony she and her young son had to survive on. The government eventually complied.[41]

As noted, in 1869 at the Constitutional Assembly in Guáimaro, the Cuban insurgency agreed to abolish the institution of slavery and to free the enslaved people in the territory they controlled. In an attempt to regain its international standing, and to win back the support of free people of color, in 1870 Spain issued the Moret Law, a plan to abolish slavery gradually by emancipating slaves over sixty and children under eleven. The law included a provision that offered freedom to slaves who fought with Spain during the war. Using the promise of freedom, both rival armies, Spanish and Cuban, attempted to convince Cubans of African descent of the benefits of fighting on their side. And, to some degree, they both succeeded. African-descended people fought under the banners of Spain and the Cuban Republic.[42] After the Moret Law was passed, women whose slaves had been confiscated, and who now wanted them back, had to face this additional hurdle, at least in the case of older slaves. In Las Tunas, the widow Ana Francisca Rivera asked the authorities to let her keep Rafaela, age sixty-three; Celedonia, twenty-six;

Emilia, sixteen; Laureana, fourteen; Inés, age three; and Cicoriano José, twenty-five. They had belonged to her husband, a rebel whose property had been confiscated. The authorities refused to comply and replied that the government's instruction left no doubt about what the fate of the slaves should be: the widow should turn in the five younger slaves, so that they would produce benefits for the Administración Depositaria. As for the slave in her sixties, the town's authority could decide what to do, in accordance with the current legislation.[43]

The war dragged on bloodily until 1878, the rebels refusing to give up their fight, gaining and losing strength as the years went by. Spain, determined not to let go of its most profitable colony, renewed its efforts after the Bourbon monarchy was restored in 1874 and sent thousands of soldiers to stop the insurrection. And so they did, forcing the rebels to accept the Pact of Zanjón, a compromise of sorts that included a plan to abolish slavery in the following years, a process that culminated in 1886.

With the end of the war, many rebels migrated to Central America, the Caribbean islands, or the United States, their property now scattered and their numbers dwindling. Between 1868 and 1878, the beginning and end of the war, Camaguey lost 20 percent of its population, the once prosperous area now being described as "a cemetery in the midst of a desert." Throughout the eastern provinces, sugar mills, country houses, and farms of all kinds were now gone, a desolation that took the region decades to overcome.[44] When the war was over, female former slaveholders from this region had to come to terms with a new social reality as they confronted poverty and destitution. Many women whose families had joined the insurrection found themselves in the novel position of having to support themselves in exile. In New York, San Salvador, San José, New Orleans, wherever they found a home, they gave music lessons, worked as seamstresses, and operated inns. The Ten Years' War had revealed the difficulties slaveholding women would face in having to fend for themselves. This was a society built on the assumption that white women's lives would be both protected by their husbands and eased by the work of their slaves. But the fact that so many Cuban women of all social and racial backgrounds ultimately sided with the anticolonial struggle, and the active role women of all backgrounds played in the wars of independence, also showed the growing status of Cuban women, particularly of the eastern provinces, as a force of change.

CONCLUSION

Between 1868 and 1878, Cubans in the eastern part of the island waged war against the Spanish government. While many of the insurgent leaders owned slaves, their economic well-being was not plantation-based but commercially derived, their financial interests clashing with the limitations imposed by colonial policies. An important strategic move to define the rebellion's superior moral standing when compared to colonial rule was to abolish slavery in the territories they controlled. And yet, as a multitude of petitions to the authorities demonstrate, women who identified with the insurgency continued to insist on their right to own slaves, and to have their slaves returned when they had been confiscated as political punishment. The women's demands are revealing: they reflect how crucial the enslaved population, even if it was simply a small number of domestic slaves, even if it was one enslaved child, was to the survival of slaveholding families; how much slaveholding women relied on their slaves not only to feed their families, but also to cook, clean, clothe, transport, and manage the household. For slave-owning women of the eastern provinces, the final abolition of slavery in 1886 brought an end to their ability to rely on enslaved workers as a source of wealth. It also brought an end to their contradictory position as both anticolonial rebels and defenders of slavery.

Conclusion

Nineteenth-century slaveholding women in Cuba came from a wide range of geographic, economic, political, ethnic, and, occasionally, even racial backgrounds. In a society where few people questioned the right of one person to own another, the institution of slavery prevailed throughout the island. Between the late 1700s and mid-1800s, nearly 700,000 men, women, and children were brought by force from Africa to work in towns, and on sugar and coffee plantations, their labor resulting in enormous profits for the slaveholding class. From the eastern and central provinces to the western ones, each region favored the type of bondage best suited to its economic needs—needs that also determined slaveholders' degree of support for the colonial status. Wealthy plantation owners, male and female, who owned large numbers of slaves counted on Spain to prevent revolts, and thus tended to defend the Spanish presence on the island. Those closer to middle-class status and who owned fewer slaves, such as cattle ranchers, small entrepreneurs, and urban dwellers, were more critical of the colonial government, many of them joining the ranks of the insurgents during the Ten Years' War.

According to Spanish law, widows and single women had control over their assets, including their slaves. With the exception of their dowry, women lost control of their property once they married, the power to manage it shifting to their husbands. And yet, despite what the legal system stipulated, married women continued to claim ownership over their contributions to the marriage, particularly their slaves. Moreover, all women could dictate their own wills without a husband's consent, a legal right that gave female slaveholders the power to voice their wishes and to influence the lives of those working for them. Their final decisions ranged from cold detachment, seen when they gave their enslaved workers to their heirs as objects, to recognition of the enslaved workers' personhood, as when they included in their wills letters of manumission or other signs and tokens of affection.

Enslaved women, men, and children eased the lives of mistresses and their families. They bought, cooked, and served slave-owning families' meals, washed and ironed their clothes, polished their floors, made their beds, breastfed and cared for their children, combed their hair, drove them around, carried the rugs on which they knelt in church, and much more. Slavery fed slaveholders and supported their lifestyle. For some, their bank balances overflowed with the phenomenal profits from the unpaid toil of the hundreds of thousands of forced laborers who worked the sugar and coffee plantations. In small and large towns, slaves were rented out, the resulting income keeping their owners either in comfort or above the poverty line.

Female slaveholders, whether immensely wealthy or just getting by, shared their male counterparts' views and ideology, their interests matching those of their fathers, husbands, and brothers. And yet, confined as they were to the domestic sphere by gender expectations, they related to the institution of slavery in a way that was distinctly female. At times the women's relationship was more distant, since often they had been sheltered from the most inhumane aspects of the plantation economy, while at times it was more personal and intense because of their constant interaction with their household slaves.

While Cuban society made no room for a female presence in the political and professional world, slavery extended mistresses' authority beyond their children, and gave them power that surpassed what was implied in a traditional mistress-servant relationship. Slaveholding women used their power, just as men did, to shape and maintain the institution of slavery.

In Havana, Santiago, Matanzas, and other towns, mistresses, in their capacity as rulers of the domestic sphere, exerted authority and influence over the household slaves. They often were the ones making the decision to buy, sell, and rent slaves; they determined their slaves' occupation and schedule, chose the clothes they wore and the food they ate, set norms of behavior and interfered in their personal lives, as they tried, more or less successfully, to impose their values on the enslaved people they owned. Mistresses attempted to "create consent"—in other words, to establish a sense of legitimacy for the status quo, while resorting to discipline when persuasion failed to succeed. Whether they were urban dwellers with domestic slaves, the absentee landladies of sugar mills who visited their properties only once a year, or coffee plantation owners who resided at the plantation, mistresses made decisions that could have life-altering effects on the lives of the people under their control.

In nineteenth-century Cuba, exploitation, racism, and fear produced an explosive situation. Relying on an enslaved work force, yet also aware of the slave rebellions that had broken out throughout the Caribbean and in Cuba itself, the slaveholding class that owned large *dotaciones* of slaves on plantations resorted to strict discipline to limit the enslaved population's ability to revolt. Slaveholding women's role—though they often fell short of fulfilling it because their upbringing made them insensitive to the plight of their slaves—was to soften the effects of that discipline. Acting as compassionate figures who cared for their slaves, mistresses occasionally alleviated slaves' pain, and in so doing helped to legitimize the notion of slavery as a benevolent institution.

Whether they were caring, malevolent, or indifferent toward those under their rule, mistresses enjoyed a position as slaveholders that provided them with authority. But the mistress-slave interaction was not simply a power relationship, it was also a human interaction filled with emotions, especially in the case of domestic slaves—the natural result of a daily coexistence and a string of encounters that often crossed generations. The *amas* were once children raised by slaves, who were owned by *amas*, and so on, and that personal connection shaped the fabric of Cuba's society and culture.

Slavery arrested the white women's ability to live an autonomous existence. Living in a patriarchal society that granted them limited educational and economic opportunities, women clung to their role as slaveholders as their lifeline; they depended on enslaved men, women, and children to provide for their families in a way they themselves were unwilling or unable to do, as illustrated by their desperate pleas to recover confiscated slaves during the Ten Years' War. And yet, losing their status as slaveholders gave them a new sense of identity. White women in large numbers fought in that war, some taking up arms against the Spanish colonial power, and they willingly faced great risks: The war forced them and their families to hide in the mountains or sent them into exile, often as widows, where they had to learn to be providers for their children.

In 1879, as the institution of slavery entered its twilight in Cuba, Pedro Gutiérrez Salazar, a Spanish liberal who had been a government official on the island, assuaged the planter class's fear of the potential revenge that could come with emancipation, by highlighting the warm relationship that existed between slaves and masters thanks to the *amas*' mediating role. Reaffirming the view of plantation mistresses as a beneficent influence, he listed the virtuous work the *señoras* had performed: they had watched over the enslaved small children, nursed the sick slaves, softened the wrath of angry overseers. Their civilizing influence had brought order, general happiness, and higher productivity.[1] In other words, the *good female slaveholder* continued to be displayed as a guarantee of future social harmony, and helped inspire what Camillia Cowling has described as the colonial power's "cozy" vision of emancipation. According to this wishful thinking, much would remain unchanged: the planter class, particularly mistresses, would continue to take care of former slaves and to be loved by them.[2] After the institution of slavery was officially abolished in 1886, the ideological defense of the status quo was forced to compete with growing nationalist ideals and the project of a "free Cuba." It was a project that pointed toward the reinvention both of women's role and of racial interactions in Cuban society, a society that would eventually look back at the notion of a "good slaveholder," male or female, as an oxymoron.

Notes

Introduction

1. Contemporary historians try to avoid the term *slave*, which conjures an objectified individual whose humanity has been diminished. While agreeing with that sentiment, I have not found a way to eliminate the term from my writing. When possible, I refer to *enslaved people* and to *enslaved men*, *women*, and *children*.

2. Moreno Fraginals, *El ingenio*, 1:262–63.

3. See Ferrer, "Cuban Slavery and Atlantic Antislavery"; and Schmidt-Nowara, *Empire and Antislavery*. For an insightful discussion of the expansion of Spain's role in the slave trade during the period when it was illegal, see Piqueras, *La Esclavitud en las Españas,* and his poignant comment that the largest numbers of slaves were brought to Cuba in the nineteenth century, a century that celebrated Reason and Liberalism (91). See also Cózar and Rodrigo y Alharilla, *Cádiz y el tráfico de esclavos*.

4. See Tomich, "The Second Slavery."

5. Voyages: The Translatlantic Slave Trade Database, accessed August 25, 2019. See also Cowling, *Conceiving Freedom*, 7; and Gott, *Cuba: A New History*, 46–47.

6. For a rich overview of American and Caribbean slaveholders' capitalist vocation, see Bassi, "Neither a Spanish nor U.S. Lake." See also Baptist, *The Half Has Never Been Told*; and Marquese, Parron, and Berbel, *Slavery and Politics*. The latter is an astute analysis of how Iberian politics affected the institution of slavery in Brazil and Cuba, and a reminder of how the planter class was pressured to keep up with technology and management strategies to improve its production in the increasingly competitive world market.

7. For a study of women's legal position in the Spanish colonies, see Arrom, *The Women of Mexico City*.

8. See Espigado, "Las Mujeres en el nuevo marco político¨; López-Cordón Cortezo, "La Situación de la mujer a finales del Antiguo Régimen."

9. Jones-Rogers, *They Were Her Property,* 126.

10. Hartman, *Lose Your Mother*, 155.

11. For a rich analysis of the often-tense interaction between the Cuban planter class and the peninsular bourgeoisie, see Moreno Fraginals, *Cuba/España*, 223–42.

12. Jones-Rogers, *They Were Her Property*, xiv–xvi.

13. Camp, *Enslaved Women*, 1.

14. Trouillot, *Silencing the Past*, 26. Some scholars of Latin American history have embraced the "archival turn," in other words, an explicit attempt to compensate for the archives' frustrating inability to illuminate the lives of the powerless. A good example is the work of La Patrona Collective, a group of Latin American historians, including Bianca Premo, David Sartorius, Jessica Delgado, and Karen Graubart, among others, whose scholarship explores ways to retrieve information about women, indigenous, and Afro-descended people through empathy, emotion, and imagination. See the issue dedicated to this topic, "Documented: The Colonial Archive and the Future of the Americas," *Hemisphere*. 27 (Winter 2018).

15. See, for example, Fradera and Schmidt-Nowara, eds., *Slavery and Antislavery in Spain's Atlantic Empire*; and the work of scholars at the Universitat Pompeu Fabra in Barcelona. See also Piqueras, *La Esclavitud en las Españas,* as well as the work of historians at the Instituto de Historia, CSIC, in Madrid.

16. Brown, "Social Death and Political Life," 1248.

Chapter 1

1. Villaverde, *Cecilia Valdés*, 55. Manuel Moreno Fraginals wrote that Cirilo Villaverde's ability to capture his society with photographic realism failed him when describing Black and mulatto characters, whose portrayal was false and distorted. Moreno Fraginals, *Cuba/España*, 306.

2. Lowell, *New Year in Cuba*, 47–48.

3. Goodman, *The Pearl of the Antilles*, 12–13.

4. Goodman, 151–52.

5. Steele, *Cuban Sketches,* 93.

6. Steele, *Cuban Sketches,* 62–63. "Sorosis," founded in New York in 1868, was the first professional women's club in the United States. Dorcas societies were charity women's groups that tended to the poor; they were usually connected to a local church.

7. Salas y Quiroga, *Viajes*, 76 (my translation).

8. Beauvallon, *La Isla de Cuba*, 102 (my translation).

9. Piron, *La Isla de Cuba*, 71–72.

10. Piron, *La Isla de Cuba*, 27–28.

11. María del Carmen Barcia Zequeira, *Oficios de mujer*, 153 (my translation).

12. Despite the narrow focus of religious schools for girls, some of them—for instance, the Ursuline nuns' school in Camaguey—turned out a whole generation of strong young women, many of whom participated in the insurgency against Spain in the 1860s. See Fernando Portuondo, *Estudios de Historia de Cuba*, 202.

13. See Prados-Torreira, *Mambisas*, 11–13, 25–26. See also María del Carmen Barcia Zequeira, *Oficios de mujer*, 153–57. Barcia provides a rich analysis and description of *escuelas de amigas* (female friends' schools), a common eighteenth- and nineteenth-century practice in which respectable (though in most cases uncredentialed) women kept schools, often in their own homes, where they taught young boys and girls basic knowledge and behavior.

14. Vinat Matas, "Colores y dolores de la educación femenina en Cuba," 108.

15. See Prados-Torreira, *Mambisas*, 25.
16. See Louis A. Perez Jr., *Intimations of Modernity*.
17. See Prados-Torreira, *Mambisas*.
18. Piron, *La Isla de Cuba*, 51 (my translation).
19. Goodman, *The Pearl of the Antilles*, 3.
20. Villaverde, *Cecilia Valdés*, 138.
21. Villaverde, *Cecilia Valdés*, 171.
22. Zambrana, *El Negro Francisco*, 85 (my translation).
23. Jones-Rogers, *They Were Her Property*, 83.
24. Cowling, *Conceiving Freedom*, 37.
25. Lowell, *New Year in Cuba*, 46.
26. Moreno Fraginals, *Cuba/España*, 208.
27. Beauvallon, *La Isla de Cuba*, 114. The American writer Mary Peabody Mann also commented on the close interaction between female slave owners and maids. In her novel *Juanita*, a fictionalized account of her two years in Cuba, a young mistress whose heart had just been broken by a suitor, dried her eyes and hid her feelings in front of her young slave, who was ready to wash her feet as usual, for fear of the slave gossiping, "for she knew that on the morrow this ontoward event would be bruited from one end of the city to the other . . . the pretty lady's maid, was the queen of gossips, and knew enough of the young mistress' affairs to make it dangerous to admit her to any confidence." Mann, *Juanita*, 24–25.
28. Green, *Remember Me to Miss Louisa*, 9.
29. For an interesting analysis of the household as the site of emotional dynamics, in this case referring to masters and servants in medieval and early modern Europe, see Broomhall, *Emotions in the Household*.
30. Camp, *Closer to Freedom*, 1–2.
31. *Diario de La Habana*, July 4, 1840: "Una negra muy robusta, humilde, sana y sin tachas, buena lavandera, regular planchadora y cocina muy bien algunos platos, en 400 ps. libres para vendedor o en 600 ps junto con su hija de 5 a 6 años, muy hábil para cuanto quieran aplicarla o también se admite cambio por una buena cocinera. Calle Obispo n.27." Alejandro de la Fuente has argued that the term *sin tachas* was meant to suggest moral integrity and should be translated as "without vices." See De la Fuente, "Slaves and the Creation of Legal Rights in Cuba." María del Carmen Barcia Zequeira has also pointed out that the term had a broad connotation and was meant to reassure the buyer that the slave had no moral vices, such as drinking, stealing, a tendency to run away, or even arrogance. Barcia Zequeira, *Oficios de mujer*, 145. I will translate *sin tacha* as "without flaws," or "without vices," depending on the context.
32. *Diario de La Habana*, 4 julio 1840: "Una negra de 20 años, de muy buena presencia, lavandera, planchadora y costurera, excelente servicial a la mano, con un negrito de dos años, sano y sin tachas, en 500 ps libres para el vendedor, también se vende sola; impondrán en la zapatería la Elegancia Habanera, calle Real de la Salud frente a la iglesia."
33. *El Redactor*, Santiago, April 29, 1850.
34. For an interesting discussion and quantitative analysis of advertisements for wet

nurses, see Franklin, *Women and Slavery in Nineteenth-Century Colonial Cuba,* 125–46. See also Barcia Zequeira, *Oficios de mujer*.

35. Fox-Genovese, *Within the Plantation Household,* 279–80.

36. *Noticiero y Lucero*, July 8, 1835: "negra nación con cría o sin ella. 15 días de parida."

37. *Noticiero y Lucero*, August 8, 1838: "tiene poco más de dos meses de parida pero se le murió la cría, joven y robusta."

38. *Diario de la Habana*, July 9, 1840: "excelente nodriza de buena y abundante leche, de carácter muy humilde, de dos meses de parida."

39. Quoted in Vann Woodward, *Mary Chesnut's Civil War*, 29.

40. Green, *Remember Me to Miss Louisa*, 42.

41. *Diario de la Habana*, July 15, 1840: "como de 22 años, propia para criandera, con su cría mulata de dos meses, de buena y abundante leche, excelente cocinera y lavandera."

42. *Diario de la Habana*, July 1, 1843: "Una negra como de 23 años de buena presencia, más que regular en batea y plancha, regular de cocina, sana y sin tacha, en 21 onzas libres para el vendedor, se da este precio por llevar hija mulata libre, de catorce meses."

43. See Perera Díaz and Meriño Fuentes, *Estrategias de libertad*, 2:30–100.

44. Moreno Fraginals, *Cuba/España*, 108.

45. *Diario de la* Habana, July 4, 1840: "Un negro joven, más que regular cocinero y zapatero de mujer, corta y hace ropa para criados, muy ágil para todo, y st en 500 ps." "Se alquila negro de 17 años, más que regular cocinero con principios de zapatero de mujer."

46. Villaverde, *Cecilia Valdés*, 100.

47. Triay, "El Calesero," in *Tipos y costumbres de la Isla de Cuba*, 109.

48. Triay, "El Calesero," in *Tipos y costumbres de la Isla de Cuba*, 110 (my translation). "Se hizo el confidente de la niña. Le llevaba cartas del novio y la llevaba en la volante, sin que lo advirtiera la vieja . . . Si el juego se descubría, podía sacar un paseo al ingenio, con exoneración de todo cargo, a menos que la voluntad de la niña pudiese tanto, que trajera la amnistía antes que la terrible sentencia hubiera causado ejecutoria."

49. Piron, *La Isla de Cuba*, 24–25 (my translation).

50. *Diario de la Habana*, July 1, 1840: "mulatica de 11 años, de bonita figura, propia para jugar con niñas y para cuanto quieran aplicarla, sana y sin tachas, en 300 ps. Libres para el vendedor."

51. *La Gaceta*, January 12, 1849: "Negro de 15 a 16 años muy ágil, humilde y acostumbrado a entretener y manejar niños."

52. *La Gaceta*, October 5, 1849: "una negrita muy ágil entendida en todo aseo de una casa y propia para entretener niños por ser muy cariñosa en 6 $ al mes, y en la misma se vende otra como de 10 años que cose muy bien y entiende en todo aseo de casa en 15 onzas libres para el vendedor, sana y st."

53. *El Siglo. Diario Político, Económico, Literario y Mercantil*, November 17, 1862: "Se alquila un mulatico como de 10 a 11 años, propio para lo que quieran alquilarlo."

54. *Diario de la Habana*, July 15, 1840: "Se vende un negrito como de 9 años, sano

y sin tachas para lo que quieran aplicarlo, por su ajuste y se solicita un mulatico que no pase de 5 o 6 años."

55. *La Gaceta*, March 30, 1849: "Se vende una mulatica de pelo propia para una niña."

56. *La Gaceta*, November 21, 1849: "Se vende mulato claro, de pelo, de buena figura, de 21 años, parece blanco."

57. Manzano, *Autobiography of a Slave / Autobiografía de un esclavo*, 45.

58. Manzano, *Autobiography*, 49.

59. Manzano, *Autobiography*, 89.

60. Manzano, *Autobiography*, 107.

61. According to Spanish law, an enslaved person was allowed to seek a new master or mistress upon obtaining permission to do so from the local authorities.

62. *La Gaceta*, May 31, 1849: "Se solicita comprar una negra general costurera y sin tachas que no esté acostumbrada a andar en la calle. Se solicita comprar un ejemplar de la Historia de España en prosa y verso por el Padre Isla, que esté en buen estado."

63. *La Gaceta*, June 20, 1849: "Se vende una negra de conducta irreprensible, cocinera de un ordinario, regular en batea y plancha, sabe coser, filetear y calar, de un mes de parida, con su cría muy sana lo mismo que ella, de buena y abundante leche, no es amiga de salir a la calle, pues aunque en ésta hay la costumbre de que lo verifiquen alguno que otro días de fiesta por las tardes, se nota en ella muy poco o ningún interés en ello."

64. *Diario de la Habana*, July 1, 1840.

65. AHPSC, Esclavos, 12.44, leg. 555, no. 10.

66. ANRC, Gobierno Superior Civil, leg. 950, no. 996000.

67. Schmidt-Nowara, *Empire and Antislavery*, 15. See also Marquese, Parron, and Berbel, *Slavery and Politics*, 187–260.

68. Perera Díaz and Meriño Fuentes, *Estrategias*, 1:198–217. For a systematic analysis of the fluctuating prices of slaves in Cuba, see Bergad, Iglesias García, and Barcia, *The Cuban Slave Market*.

69. See Marquese, Parron, and Berbel, *Slavery and Politics*, 224–25.

70. Marquese, Parron, and Berbel, *Slavery and Politics*, 209–17.

71. Testamento de Teresa O'Farrill, ANRC, Donativos y Remisiones, 1823–24, Caja no. 327, no. Orden 3.

72. Testamento de Josefa Antonia González, BNJM, CM, Sociedad T. 28 no.12–55.

73. Doña Josefa Reyna, BNJM, CM, Pérez n. 689.

74. Cowling, *Conceiving Freedom*, 27.

75. Hevia Lanier, "Historias escondidas." See also Hevia Lanier, "Historias ocultas."

76. Goodman, *The Pearl of the Antilles*, 37–38.

77. See for instance, "El moreno Joaquín Aguirre de doña María del Rosario Alentado se queja del excesivo jornal que se le exige," Havana, May 29, 1843, ARNC, Gobierno Superior Civil, leg. 941, no. 99229.

78. See de la Fuente, "Slaves and the Creation of Legal Rights in Cuba," 101–33.

79. De la Fuente, "Slaves and the Creation of Legal Rights in Cuba," 106.

80. Perera Díaz and Meriño Fuentes, *Estrategias*, 1:299–300.

81. Scott, *Emancipation in Cuba*, 74.

82. Perera Díaz and Meriño Fuentes remind us of E. P. Thompson's argument that one of the conditions for a legal system to be effective is the appearance of being fair (*Estrategias*, 1:3). See also Cowling, *Conceiving Freedom*, 62. Cowling reminds us not to think of *síndicos* necessarily as the slaves' champions, but rather as professionals performing a job, with a range of positions on abolition, some in favor, some against it.

83. La negra Cecilia se queja del maltrato de su ama doña Inés Hernández, ANRC, Gobierno Superior Civil, leg. 949, no. 3356.

84. See Perera Díaz and Meriño Fuentes's section on prostitution as a strategy that enslaved women could rely on to gain freedom (*Estrategias*, 2:100–119).

85. Moreno Fraginals, *Cuba/España*, 102.

86. *Cédula amos esclavos no exijan demasiado rigor pago jornal*, 1749, BNJM, CM Bachiller no. 573.

87. For more information on *depósitos*, see Cowling, *Conceiving Freedom*, 62.

88. Dña Sebastiana Puig de Moré en queja del procedimiento del Síndico Betancourt respecto de su esclava Salomé, ANRC, Gobierno Superior Civil, leg. 967, no. 94176.

89. ANRC, GSC, leg. 959, no. 33644.

90. Carta de Libertad, AHPSC, Protocolo: 39, fol. 109.

91. Carta de Libertad, AHPSC, Protocolo: fol. 116v.

Chapter 2

1. Two decades later, when Samuel Hazard, an American artist and writer traveled throughout the island sketching and writing about what he saw, he repeated the same theme, with one of his illustrations including two white women being served refreshments inside a boiling house. Hazard, *Cuba with Pen and Pencil*, 542.

2. Villaverde, *Cecilia Valdés*, 373.

3. Zambrana, *El negro Francisco*, 112 (my translation).

4. Ely, *Cuando reinaba su majestad el azúcar*, 194.

5. Zambrana, *El negro Francisco*, 109 (my translation).

6. Quoted in Howe, *Articulate Sisters*, 128.

7. Suárez y Romero, "Ingenios," in *Colección de Artículos*, 198. All translations of articles from this collection are my own.

8. Morales Pérez, introduction to García, *La Esclavitud desde la esclavitud*, xviii (my translation).

9. Suárez y Romero, "La Casa del Trapiche," in *Colección de Artículos*, 219.

10. Suárez y Romero, "El Corte de Caña," in *Colección de Artículos*, 225–31.

11. Schmidt-Nowara, *Empire and Antislavery*, 32–33.

12. Moreno Fraginals, *Cuba/España*, 227 (my translation).

13. Villaverde, *Cecilia Valdés*, 356.

14. Suárez y Romero, "Los Domingos en los Ingenios," in *Colección de Artículos*, 208.

15. Suárez y Romero, "La Casa del Trapiche," in *Colección de Artículos*, 220.

16. Manzano, *The Autobiography of a Slave. Autobiografía de un esclavo*, 45.

17. Suárez y Romero, "Su Retrato," in *Colección de Artículos*, 84.

18. As Christopher Schmidt-Nowara and Camillia Cowling have shown, the notion

that women brought "moral authority to society" was deployed by the Spanish Abolitionist Society to encourage the female population to support the antislavery cause. Schmidt-Nowara, *Empire and Slavery*, 92; Cowling, *Conceiving Freedom*, 110–11.

19. See Espigado, "Las Mujeres en el nuevo marco político," 39. See also Claret, *Sermones de misión.*

20. See Marquese, Parron, and Berbel, *Slavery and Politics*, 200–201.

21. Santa Cruz y Montalvo, *Viaje a la Habana*, Letter III, 96 (my translation).

22. Villaverde, *Cecilia Valdés*, 304.

23. Villaverde, *Cecilia Valdés*, 296.

24. Gómez de Avellaneda, *Sab*, 57.

25. Suárez y Romero, *Francisco,* 163–64.

26. Suárez y Romero, *Francisco,* 160.

27. David Turnbull, quoted in Ely, *Cuando reinaba su majestad el azúcar*, 47–48. Turnbull replaced Richard Madden as British consul. Both officials fought to make Spain abide by the anti–slave trade agreements it had signed and were active participants in del Monte's abolitionist circle. See Marquese, Parron, and Berbel, *Slavery and Politics,* 192.

28. Tanco Bosmeniel, *Petrona y Rosalía.*

29. Zambrana, *El Negro Francisco*, 3.

30. Saco, *La historia de la esclavitud desde los tiempos más remotos hasta nuestros días*, 3:145–46, 409.

31. Villaverde, *Cecilia Valdés*, 335.

32. De la Fuente, "Sugar and Slavery in Early Colonial Cuba," 144.

33. BNJM, CM, Sociedad varios T 6, no. 17.

34. Ortiz, *Los Negros esclavos*, 275.

35. Quoted in García, *Voices of the Enslaved*, 47–54.

36. Ferrer, *Freedom's Mirror*, 26–27.

37. García, *Voices of the Enslaved,* 55–73.

38. Duque de Estrada, Antonio Nicolás. *Doctrina Cristiana acomodada a la capacidad de los negros bozales,* Edición Bachiller, BNJM, 2006.

39. Paquette, *Sugar Is Made with Blood*, 62.

40. Pichardo, *Documentos*, 1:318–26.

41. García, *Voices of the Enslaved*, 15. See also Eugene Genovese's *Roll, Jordan, Roll*, in which he argues that slaveholders in the American South relied on paternalism to help them justify the system of slavery while also easing tensions between the enslaver and the enslaved on the plantation.

42. Howe, ed., *Articulate Sisters*, 131–32.

43. Abbott, *Letters Written in the Interior of Cuba*, 145.

44. Abbott, *Letters Written in the Interior of Cuba*, 164–65.

45. Abbott, *Letters Written in the Interior of Cuba*, 36.

46. Ferrer, *Freedom's Mirror*, 12–13.

47. Howe, ed., *Articulate Sisters*, 128–29.

48. Howe, ed., *Articulate Sisters*, 131.

49. Bremer, *The Homes of the New World*, 2:290.

50. Bremer, *The Homes of the New World*, 2:303.

51. Bremer, *The Homes of the New World*, 2:332.

52. Bremer, *The Homes of the New World*, 2:332.

53. Bremer, *The Homes of the New World*, 2:408.

54. Suárez y Romero, "La llegada al ingenio," 1863, BNJM, CM Suarez R. T. 6, no. 28, 268–70 (my translation).

55. Hartman, *Lose Your Mother*, 87.

56. Bremer, *Homes of the New World*, 2:351.

57. Glymph, *Out of the House of Bondage*. Glymph is referring, among others, to works such as Catherine Clinton's *The Plantation Mistress*.

58. Glymph, *Out of the House of Bondage*, 40.

59. Villaverde, *Cecilia Valdés*, 345.

60. Santa Cruz y Montalvo, Condesa de Merlín, Letter XXV, *Viajeras al Caribe*, 135 (my translation).

61. Santa Cruz y Montalvo, Carta XV, *Viajeras al Caribe*, 117.

62. Castillo, "La Mujer Cubana," 116–17 (my tranlation).

63. Atkins, *Sixty Years in Cuba*, 95–96. See also Scott, "A Cuban Connection." Scott argues that, by the 1880s, the knowledge that slaves, like the ones on Atkins's plantation, had of their imminent freedom contributed to their rebelliousness.

64. Bremer, *Homes of the New World*, 351.

Chapter 3

1. Guerra Sánchez, *Mudos Testigos*, 65.

2. As an example, see Hazard, *Cuba with Pen and Pencil*, 334–45.

3. Quoted in Pérez de la Riva, *El Café*, 135–36 (my translation).

4. Lowell, *New Year in Cuba*, 76–78.

5. Van Norman Jr., *Shade-Grown Slavery*, 31.

6. See Singleton, *Slavery behind the Wall*.

7. The Sage and Lowell families counted George DeWolfe, from Rhode Island, among their friends. DeWolfe is an example of an American planter in Cuba who had been a slave trader. See Singleton, *Slavery behind the Wall*, 39.

8. Lowell, *A New Year in Cuba*, 78.

9. Lowell, *A New Year in Cuba*, 69.

10. Lowell, *A New Year in Cuba*, 79. For studies on slave revolts on Cuban plantations in the 1840s, see Van Norman Jr., *Shade-Grown Slavery;* and, especially, Finch, *Rethinking Slave Rebellion in Cuba;* and Reid-Vázquez, *The Year of the Lash*.

11. Lowell, *A New Year in Cuba*, 79.

12. Lowell, *A New Year in Cuba*, 92–93.

13. Lowell, *A New Year in Cuba*, 94. In some sugar mills the masters added salted meat or cod to *funche*, ingredients that likely helped the enslaved labor force feel more satiated. Moreno Fraginals, *El Ingenio*, 2:58.

14. Lowell, *A New Year in Cuba*, 105.

15. Pérez de la Riva, *El Café*, 126.

16. Van Norman Jr., *Shade-Grown Slavery*, 70.

17. Barcia, *Seeds of Insurrection*, 32.

18. Mann, *Juanita*, 223.

19. Mann, *Juanita*, 48. John C. Havard has pointed out that Mann turned Helen Wentworth into a symbol of an idealized American liberalism that helped celebrate US nationalism. Havard, *Hispanicism and Early US Literature*, 119–45.

20. Mann, *Juanita*, 30.

21. Mann, *Juanita*, 35–36.

22. Mann, *Juanita*, 79.

23. Lora Alvarez, "Fisonomía de un cafetal francés"; Lora Alvarez, "Los Antiguos cafetales francohaitianos."

24. Hazard, *Cuba with Pen and Pencil*, 467.

25. Lora Alvarez, "Fisonomía de un cafetal francés."

26. Portuondo Zúñiga, "El Paraíso de Luisa Girard de Heredia," 10. Luisa Girard is the same person as María Luisa Girard.

27. Portuondo Zúñiga, "El Paraíso de Luisa Girard de Heredia," 19.

28. Portuondo Zúñiga, "El Paraíso de Luisa Girard de Heredia," 19.

29. Beauvallon, *La Isla de Cuba*, 282 (my translation).

30. Beauvallon, *La Isla de Cuba*, 286.

31. Beauvallon, *La Isla de Cuba*, 288.

32. Beauvallon, *La Isla de Cuba*, 292.

33. Portuondo Zuñiga, "El Paraíso de Luisa Girard," 15.

34. Masters had the option of granting their last name to slaves who had belonged to their family for a long time, or of whom they were particularly fond. Most slaves had no last name as they had no legal or civil identity.

35. The gourds' tough skin and durability, their edible meat and seeds, as well as their usefulness as a utensil when dried, made them a welcome acquisition in any poor household.

36. In the context of a patriarchal society such as this one, it is not surprising that masters, and particularly mistresses, would view the enslaved families' abilities to reproduce and thrive as a positive reflection upon themselves. High birth rates among the enslaved seemed to validate the notion that mistresses were good mothers who took care of their charges.

37. Portuondo Zuñiga, "El Paraíso de Luisa Girard," 20.

38. Fajardo, "La familia Stable Bonne."

39. Bremer, *The Homes of the New World*, 398.

40. Piron, *La Isla de Cuba*, 55 (my translation).

41. Piron, *La Isla de Cuba*, 126. For an analysis of the role of the *coartación* system in rural Cuba, see Van Norman Jr., *Shade-Grown Slavery*, 118. He claims that the opportunity to benefit from that system depended on access to the economy, which was greater at a *cafetal* than at an *ingenio*, but concludes that even at coffee plantations, the number of slaves able to free themselves was limited.

42. Singleton, *Slavery behind the Wall*, 167.

43. Piron, *La Isla de Cuba*, 127 (my translation).

44. Goodman, *The Pearl of the Antilles*, 196–97.

45. Goodman, *The Pearl of the Antilles*, 199.

Chapter 4

1. The title of "don" or "doña," always preceding the name, in nineteenth-century Cuban society was used to signify a person's social standing and whiteness.

2. Testamento de María Luisa Dinet, AHPSC, Fondo Juzgado de Primera Instancia, leg. 603, no. 1.

3. My selection of wills has been based on a combination of factors: first, access to them at the José Martí National Library, the National Archive in Havana, and the Provincial Archive of Santiago. Second, my choices are meant to reflect the dialogue between my narrative and the primary sources I encountered. I have attempted to include testaments signed by women from a variety of social backgrounds, though affluent women's wills were easier to locate for obvious reasons, and testaments that capture the range of choices they had when considering their legacy. Every time I read a will—fragile, at times undecipherable, documents as they are—I felt thrilled to be able to include another small piece of the puzzle that constitutes Cuban women's past. Unless otherwise noted, all translations from the wills are my own.

4. Arrom, *The Women of Mexico City*, 61.

5. ANRC, Audiencia de Santiago de Cuba, leg. 63, no.1573.

6. Testamento de dña. Teresa Beltrán de Santa Cruz, Viuda del Conde San Juan de Jaruco, BNJM, CM, Pérez, no. 674.

7. Testamento de Bernarda de Arango, BNJM, CM, Pérez, no. 657.

8. Testamento de María del Carmen Sotolengo Alfaro, BNJM, CM, Pérez, no. 692.

9. Testamento de María Caridad Méndez, APSC, Fondo Juzgado Primera Instancia, leg. 551, no. 2: "*amortajada humildemente con cruz alta, capa de oro y ocho acompañados.*"

10. Testamento de dña. Josefa Reyna, BNJM, CM, Pérez, no. 689.

11. "Autos testamentarios formados de los bienes que quedaron por fallecimiento de doña Bárbara María Pérez," AHPSC, leg. 553, no. 3.

12. Arrom, *The Women of Mexico City*, 63.

13. Testamento de María Caridad Méndez, ARSC, Fondo Juzgado Primera Instancia, leg. 551, no. 2.

14. "Testamento. Escribano de Cabildo: Antonio Martínez: Año: 1846," AHPSC, Protocolo, no. 39.

15. "Testamento. Escribano de Cabildo: Antonio Martínez: Año: 1846."

16. Testamento de dña. Josefa Reyna, BNJM, CM, Pérez, no. 689.

17. Testamento de María del Rosario González y Mildres, BNJM, CM, Pérez, no. 691.

18. Testamento de María Caridad Méndez, AHPSC, Fondo Juzgado Primera Instancia, leg. 551, no. 2.

19. Testamento de María Caridad Méndez.

20. Testamento de María de los Angeles Rodríguez Gálvez (1862), BNJM, CM, Pérez, no. 703.

21. Testamento de Josefa Rodríguez Morilla, BNJM, CM, Pérez, no. 722.

22. Testamento de don Matías Bernal, AHPSC, leg. 574, no. 2.

23. Testamento de dña. Teresa Beltrán de Santa Cruz, Viuda del Conde San Juan de Jaruco, BNJM, CM, Pérez, no. 674.

24. Testamento de María de los Angeles Rodríguez Gálvez, BNJM, CM, Pérez, no. 703.

25. Fuentes, *Dispossessed Lives*, 92.

26. Testamento de María de los Angeles Rodríguez Gálvez, BNJM, CM, Pérez, no. 703.

27. Testamento de Bernarda de Arango, BNJM, CM, Pérez, no. 657.

28. Colonial authorities considered the practice of freeing slaves after the owner's death as unwise: Captain General Concha argued in 1856 that Spanish and Creole slaveholders were too good to their slaves, who were not prepared for their freedom. Quoted in Perera Díaz and Meriño Fuentes, *Estrategias,* 1:103.

29. Broomhall, *Emotions in the Household*, 121–22.

30. Hevia Lanier, "Historias ocultas," 45.

31. I am indebted to art historian Maciel Reyes Aguilar, at the Universidad de Oriente, for pointing this out to me.

32. Testamento de Inés González de Carbajal, BNJM, CM, Bachiller, no. 854.

33. Testamento de Bernarda de Arango, BNJM, CM, Pérez, no. 657.

34. Testamento de María del Carmen Sotolengo Alfaro, BNJM, CM, Pérez, no. 692.

35. "Testamento de dña. Teresa Beltrán de Santa Cruz, Viuda del Conde San Juan de Jaruco," BNJM, CM, Pérez, no. 674.

36. Testamento de Lucía Dunand, AHPSC, leg. 180, no. 4051.

37. Testamento de Magdalena Petit, ANC, Audiencia de Santiago de Cuba, leg. 551.

38. "Testamento de María Ignacia de Contreras, Marquesa viuda de San Felipe y Santiago," BNJM, CM, Pérez, no. 672.

39. Camp, *Enslaved Women*, 2.

40. "Testamento de la Condesa Viuda de Casa Montalvo," BNJM, CM, Bachiller, no. 426.

41. "Testamento de dña. Teresa Beltrán de Santa Cruz."

42. "Testamento Teresa Goumee. Escribano de Cabildo: Antonio Martínez," AHPSC, Protocolo, no. 39.

43. Testamento de Manuela Pérez, BNJM, CM, Bachiller, no. 195.

44. Quoted in Marrero, *Cuba, economía y sociedad azúcar, ilustración y conciencia*, 9:17.

45. Testamento de doña Josefa Reyna, BNJM, CM, Pérez, no. 689.

46. "Autos testamentarios formados de los bienes que quedaron por fallecimiento de doña Bárbara María Pérez," AHPSC, leg. 553, no. 3.

47. División de Bienes, doña Josefa Ramírez y Morilla, BNJM, CM, Pérez, no. 722.

48. "Testamento de los cónyuges Irino Linares and Margarita Ramos hecho a favor de sus hijos. Incluye donación de esclavos," ANRC, Fondo Donativos y Remisiones, leg. 526, no. 2.

49. "Josefa Antonia González viuda albacea de D Santiago Massana," BNJM, CM, Sociedad T. 28, nos. 12–55.

50. "Autos testamentarios formados de los bienes que quedaron por fallecimiento de doña Bárbara María Pérez."

51. Already in the early 1700s there are records of women acting as godmothers of slave children. When, in 1706, the priest Tiburcio Oña finished baptizing the daughter of a white couple, the girl's godmother, doña María de la Leche Núñez, asked him to

accompany her to her own home, so that he could also baptize one of her slaves, a girl born a few weeks earlier, whose godmother she became and who was also named María de la Leche. See Bautizo dos niñas, BNJM, CM, Pérez, no. 564.

52. Testamento de Elena Ducté, ANRC, Audiencia de Santiago de Cuba, leg. 63, no. 1573. Rachel O'Toole has argued that it was not unusual for slaveholding women in colonial Latin America to embrace mixed-race children as a way to reaffirm the white woman's authority while diminishing the power of the real mother. She also argues that invoking "good service" when freeing an enslaved servant could be a coded way to acknowledge family ties between the master or mistress and the manumitted slave. O'Toole, "Slavery, Freedom, and Intimate Obedience in Colonial Peru."

53. Testamento de María Caridad Méndez, APSC, Fondo Juzgado Primera Instancia, leg. 551, no. 2.

54. Testamento de Manuela Pérez, BNJM, CM, Bachiller, no. 195.

55. Testamento de doña Inés González de Carbajal, BNJM, CM, Bachiller, no. 854.

56. Prudencio Casamayor, one of the first French refugees from Saint Domingue to buy land in Sierra Maestra, had become a Spanish citizen in 1803, and hispanized his last name. Before the trade became illegal, Casamayor had been a slave trader.

57. "Angela Casamayor. Año: 1853," AHPSC, no. 46.

Chapter 5

1. Guerra Sánchez, *La Guerra de los 10 Años*, 1:215.

2. See Moreno Fraginals, *Cuba/España*, 270.

3. See Llaverías, "*El Consejo Administrativo de Bienes Embargados*," for an impassioned overview of the impact the confiscations had on the insurrectionists.

4. See Ferrer, *Insurgent Cuba*. See also Piqueras, *La Esclavitud en las Españas*, 234–42.

5. Stoler, *Along the Archival Grain*, 1–2.

6. Moreno Fraginals, *Cuba/España*, 99 (my translation).

7. Guerra Sánchez, *La Guerra de los Diez Años*, 1:219–31; Llaverías, "El Consejo Administrativo de Bienes Embargados."

8. Quoted in Moreno Fraginals, *Cuba/España*, 276 (my translation).

9. Pichardo, *Documentos para la historia de Cuba*, 1:379.

10. Sartorius, *Ever Faithful*, 95.

11. AHN, Ultramar, leg. 4352, no. 72.

12. Quoted in Cento Gómez, *Nadie Puede Ser Indiferente*, 163 (my translation).

13. Cento Gómez, *Nadie Puede Ser Indiferente*, 164.

14. AHN, Ultramar, leg. 4773, no. 42.

15. AHN, Ultramar, leg. 4343 S (1–32), no. 6.

16. AHN, Ultramar, leg. 4352, no. 66.

17. AHN, Ultramar, leg. 4352, no. 103.

18. AHN, Ultramar, leg. 4352, no. 51.

19. AHN, Ultramar, leg. 4352, no. 7.

20. Fuentes, *Dispossessed Lives*, 92.

21. AHN, Ultramar, leg. 4352, no. 96.

22. AHN, Ultramar, leg. 4352, no. 50.

23. AHN, Ultramar, leg. 4352, no. 1.

24. AHN, Ultramar, leg. 4352 no.100.

25. AHN, Ultramar, leg. 4343, no. 31.

26. Quoted in Cento Gómez and Muñoz Gutiérrez, *Salvador Cisneros Betancourt*, 33.

27. AHN, Ultramar, leg. 4352, no. 67.

28. AHN, Ultramar, leg. 4352, no. 90.

29. AHN, Ultramar, leg. 4352, no. 88.

30. AHN, Ultramar, leg. 4352, no.101.

31. AHN, Ultramar, leg. 4352, no. 93.

32. Cento Gómez, *Nadie Puede Ser Indiferente*, 207.

33. Quoted in Cento Gómez and Muñoz Gutiérrez, *Salvador Cisneros Betancourt*, 28–29. See also Ferrer, *Insurgent Cuba*.

34. Ferrer, *Insurgent Cuba*, 47.

35. González Sedeño, *La Vida pública y secreta de Encarnación Varona*, 128–46.

36. Cento Gómez, *Nadie puede ser indiferente*, 154.

37. Cento Gómez, *Nadie puede ser indiferente*, 153–54.

38. For an original analysis of the role of race during the Ten Years' War, see Sartorius, *Ever Faithful*.

39. Moreno Fraginals, *Cuba/España*, 281.

40. Quoted in Gómez Véliz, "La Mujer en el Fondo Consejo Administrativo de Bienes Embargados a Infidentes," 3. Other examples, including cases from the Archivo Histórico Provincial de Granma, can be found in Torres Elers, *María Cabrales*.

41. AHN, Ultramar, leg. 4774, no. 68.

42. See Sartorius, *Ever Faithful*, 94–127. See also Piqueras, *La Esclavitud en las Españas*, 242–51.

43. AHN, Ultramar, leg. 4352, no. 23.

44. Guerra Sánchez, *La Guerra de los Diez Años*, 344.

Conclusion

1. Gutiérrez Salazar, *Reformas de Cuba*, 12–13.

2. Cowling, *Conceiving Freedom*, 156.

Bibliography

Archives

Madrid, Spain

Archivo Histórico Nacional (AHN)

Sección de Estado; Sección de Ultramar.

Havana, Cuba

Archivo Nacional de la República de Cuba (ANRC)

Audiencia de Santiago de Cuba

Donativos y Remisiones

Biblioteca Nacional de Cuba José Martí (BNJM)

Colección Manuscritos (CM) Bachiller; Pérez; Sociedad; Duque; Suárez; Raros y Valiosos.

Santiago de Cuba, Cuba

Archivo Histórico Provincial de Santiago de Cuba (AHPSC)

Fondo de Juzgado de Primera Instancia

Protocolo

Autos Testamentarios

Periodicals

Diario de la Habana

La Gaceta

Noticiero y Lucero

El Redactor

El Siglo. Diario político, económico, literario y mercantil

Published Books and Articles

Abbott, Abiel. *Letters Written in the Interior of Cuba, between the Mountains of Arcana, to the East, and of Cusco, to the West, in the Months of February, March, April, and May, 1828*. Boston: Bowles & Dearborn, 1829.

Aimes, Hubert H. S. *A History of Slavery in Cuba 1511 to 1865*. New York: G. P. Putnam's Sons, Knickerbocker Press, 1907.

Araújo, Nara, ed. *Viajeras al Caribe*. Havana: Casa de las Américas, 1983.

Arrom, Silvia Marina. *The Women of Mexico City, 1790–1857*. Stanford, CA: Stanford University Press, 1985.

Atkins, Edwin Farnsworth. *Sixty Years in Cuba: Reminiscences of Edwin F. Atkins*. Cambridge, MA: Riverside Press, 1926.

Bachiller y Morales, Antonio, ed. *Tipos y costumbres de la isla de Cuba. Colección de artículos por los mejores autores de este género. Obra ilustrada por D. Víctor Patricio Landaluze*. Havana: Miguel de Villa, 1881. Colección Facsímil Libros Raros y Valiosos, BNJM, 2010.

Baptist, Edward E. *The Half Has Never Been Told: Slavery and the Making of American Capitalism*. New York: Basic Books, 2014.

Barcia, Manuel. *Seeds of Insurrection: Domination and Resistance on Western Cuban Plantations*. Baton Rouge: Louisiana State University Press, 2012.

Barcia Zequeira, María del Carmen. *Oficios de mujer. Parteras, nodrizas y "amigas." Servicios públicos en espacios privados (siglo XVII–siglo XIX)*. Santiago de Cuba: Editorial Oriente, 2015.

Bassi, Ernesto. "Neither a Spanish nor U.S. Lake: The Caribbean, A Region in Its Own Right." *American Historian* 16 (May 2018): 27–33.

Beauvallon, Jean-Baptiste Rosamond de. *La Isla de Cuba. Primera parte. Viaje a La Habana, a las costas, al interior, a Santiago. Sociedad–costumbres–paisajes–episodios*. 1844. Translated by Francisco Díaz Solar. Santiago de Cuba: Editorial Oriente, 2002.

Bergad, Laird W., Fe Iglesias García, and María del Carmen Barcia. *The Cuban Slave Market 1790–1880*. Cambridge: Cambridge University Press, 1995.

Bremer, Fredrika. *The Homes of the New World. Impressions of America*, vol. 2. Translated by Mary Howitt. 1853. New York: Negro Universities Press, 1968.

Broomhall, Susan, ed. *Emotions in the Household, 1200–1900*. Houndsmill, UK: Palgrave Macmillan, 2008.

Brown, Vincent. "Social Death and Political Life in the Study of Slavery." *American Historical Review* 114, no. 5 (December 2009): 1248.

Calcagno, Francisco. *Romualdo, uno de tantos*. Havana: Imprenta El Pilar, 1891.

Camp, Stephanie M. H. *Closer to Freedom: Enslaved Women and Everyday Resistance in the Plantation South*. Chapel Hill: University of North Carolina Press, 2004.

Castillo, Aurelia del. "La Mujer Cubana." In *Escritos de Aurelia Castillo de González*. Havana: Siglo XX, 1918.

Cento Gómez, Elda. *Nadie puede ser indiferente. Mirada a las guerras (1868–1898)*. Santiago de Cuba: Editorial Oriente, 2013.

Cento Gómez, Elda, and Ricardo Muñoz Gutiérrez. *Salvador Cisneros Betancourt. Entre la controversia y la fe*. Havana: Editorial de Ciencias Sociales, 2009.

Claret, Antonio María. *Sermones de misión*. Barcelona: Librería Religiosa, 1858.

Clinton, Catherine. *The Plantation Mistress: Woman's World in the Old South*. New York: Pantheon Books, 1982.

Corwin, Arthur F. *Spain and the Abolition of Slavery in Cuba (1817–1886)*. Austin:

University of Texas Press for the Institute of Latin American Studies, 1967.

Cowling, Camillia. *Conceiving Freedom: Women of Color, Gender, and the Abolition of Slavery in Havana and Rio de Janeiro*. Chapel Hill: University of North Carolina Press, 2013.

Cózar, Maria del Carmen, and Martín Rodrigo y Alharilla, eds. *Cádiz y el tráfico de esclavos. De la legalidad a la clandestinidad*. Madrid: Sílex, 2018.

De la Fuente, Alejandro. "Slaves and the Creation of Legal Rights in Cuba: *Coartación* and *Papel*." In *Slavery and Antislavery in Spain's Atlantic Empire*, ed. Josep M. Fradera and Christopher Schmidt-Nowara, 101–33. New York: Berghahn Books, 2013.

———. "Sugar and Slavery in Early Colonial Cuba." In *Tropical Babylons: Sugar and the Making of the Atlantic World, 1450–1680*, ed. Stuart B. Schwartz, 115–57. Chapel Hill: University of North Carolina Press, 2004.

Duque de Estrada, Antonio Nicolás. *Doctrina Cristiana acomodada a la capacidad de los negros bozales*.1796. Facsimile of original (original in safe). Edición Bachiller, BNJM, 2006.

Durán, María Angeles Heras, Rosa María Capel Martínez, et al. *Mujer y sociedad en España*. Madrid: Ministerio de Cultura, Dirección General de la Juventud y Promoción Socio-Cultural, 1986.

Ely, Roland T. *Cuando reinaba su majestad el azúcar. Estudio histórico-sociológico de una tragedia latinoamericana. El monocultivo en Cuba, origen y evolución del proceso*. Buenos Aires: Editorial Sudamericana, 1963.

Espigado, Gloria. "Las Mujeres en el nuevo marco político." In *Historia de las mujeres en España y América Latina. Del siglo XIX a los umbrales del XX*, ed. Isabel Morant, vol. 3, 27–60. Madrid: Cátedra, 2006.

Ferrer, Ada. "Cuban Slavery and Antislavery." In *Slavery and Antislavery in Spain's Atlantic Empire*, ed. Josep M. Fradera and Christopher Schmidt-Nowara, 134–57. New York: Berghahn Books, 2013.

———. *Freedom's Mirror: Cuba and Haiti in the Age of Revolution*. New York: Cambridge University Press, 2014.

———. *Insurgent Cuba: Race, Nation, and Revolution, 1868–1898*. Chapel Hill: University of North Carolina Press, 1999.

Finch, Aisha. *Rethinking Slave Rebellion in Cuba: La Escalera and the Insurgencies of 1841–1844*. Chapel Hill: University of North Carolina Press, 2015.

Fox-Genovese, Elizabeth. *Within the Plantation Household: White Women of the Old South*. Chapel Hill: University of North Carolina Press, 1988.

Fradera, Josep M., and Christopher Schmidt-Nowara, eds. *Slavery and Antislavery in Spain's Atlantic Empire*. New York: Berghahn Books, 2013.

Franklin, Sarah L. *Women and Slavery in Nineteenth-Century Colonial Cuba*. Rochester, NY: University of Rochester Press, 2012.

Fuentes, Marissa J. *Dispossessed Lives: Enslaved Women, Violence and the Archive*. Philadelphia: University of Pennsylvania Press, 2016.

Garcia, Gloria. *La Esclavitud desde la Esclavitud*. Havana: Editorial de Ciencias Sociales, 2003.

———. *Voices of the Enslaved in Nineteenth-Century Cuba: A Documentary History.* Translated by Nancy Westrate. Chapel Hill: University of North Carolina Press, 2011.

Genovese, Eugene. *Roll, Jordan, Roll: The World the Slaves Made.* 2d ed. New York: Vintage Books, 1976.

Glymph, Thavolia. *Out of the House of Bondage: The Transformation of the Plantation Household.* Cambridge: Cambridge University Press, 2008.

Gómez de Avellaneda, Gertrudis. *Sab.* Translated and edited by Nina M. Scott. Austin: University of Texas Press, 1993.

Gómez Véliz, Doneya. "La Mujer en el Fondo Consejo Administrativo de Bienes Embargados a Infidentes. Una muestra documental." *Boletín del Archivo Nacional de la República de Cuba* 15 (2005): 1–8.

González Sedeño, Modesto. *La Vida pública y secreta de Encarnación de Varona.* Havana: Centro de Investigación y Desarrollo de la Cultura Cubana Juan Marinello, 2004.

Goodman, Walter. *The Pearl of the Antilles, or An Artist in Cuba.* London: Henry S. King, 1873.

Gott, Richard. *Cuba: A New History.* New Haven, CT: Yale University Press, 2004.

Green, Sharony. *Remember Me to Miss Louisa: Hidden Black-White Intimacies in Antebellum America.* DeKalb: Northern Illinois University Press, 2015.

Guerra Sánchez, Ramiro. *Guerra de los 10 Años.* 2 vols. Havana: Editorial de Ciencias Sociales, 1972.

———. *Mudos Testigos. Crónica del ex-cafetal Jesús Nazareno.* Havana: Editorial Lex, 1948.

Gutiérrez y Salazar, Pedro. *Reformas de Cuba. Cuestión social.* Madrid: Imprenta de Manuel G. Hernández, 1879.

Hartman, Saidiya. *Lose Your Mother: A Journey along the Atlantic Slave Route.* New York: Farrar, Straus, 2007.

Havard, John C. *Hispanicism and Early US Literature: Spain, Mexico, Cuba, and the Origins of US National Identity.* Tuscaloosa: University of Alabama Press, 2018.

Hazard, Samuel. *Cuba with Pen and Pencil.* Hartford, CT: Hartford Publishing Co., 1871.

Hevia Lanier, Oilda. "Historias escondidas: Mujeres negras dueñas de esclavosen la Habana colonial (1800–1860)." *Revolución y Cultura* (February, 2016): 49–57.

———. "Historias ocultas. Mujeres negras dueñas de esclavos en la Habana colonial (1800–1860)." In *Emergiendo del silencio. Mujeres negras en la historia de Cuba*, ed. Oilda Hevia Lanier and Daisy Rubiera Castillo, 3–56. Havana: Editorial Ciencias Sociales, 2016.

Howe, M. A. DeWolde, ed. *Articulate Sisters: Passages from Journals and Letters of the Daughters of President Josiah Quincy of Harvard University.* Cambridge, MA: Harvard University Press, 1946.

Jones-Rogers, Stephanie E. *They Were Her Property: White Women as Slave Owners in the American South.* New Haven, CT: Yale University Press, 2019.

Knight, Franklin W. *The Caribbean: The Genesis of a Fragmented Nationalism.* 2d ed. New York: Oxford University Press, 1990.

Llaverías, Joaquín. *"El Consejo Administrativo de Bienes Embargados." Discurso solemne a la Academia de la Historia de Cuba. 10 de octubre*. Havana: Academia de la Historia, 1941.

López-Cordón Cortezo, María Victoria. "La Situación de la mujer a finales del Antiguo Régimen (1760–1860.)" In *Mujer y sociedad en España, 1700–1975*, ed. María Angeles Heras and Rosa María Capel Martínez, 47–95. Madrid: Dirección General de Juventud y Promoción Social, 1982.

Lora Alvarez, Marta E. "Fisonomía de un cafetal francés." *Revista de Caribe* 4, no. 10 (1987): 89–91.

Lowell, Mary Gardner. *New Year in Cuba: Mary Gardner Lowell's Travel Diary, 1831–1832*. Edited with introduction by Karen Roberts. Boston: Massachusetts Historical Society and Northeastern University Press, 2003.

Mann, Mary Peabody. *Juanita: A Romance of Real Life in Cuba Fifty Years Ago*. Edited and with introduction by Patricia M. Ard. Charlottesville: University Press of Virginia, 2000.

Manzano, Juan Francisco. *Autobiography of a Slave / Autobiografía de un esclavo*. Bilingual edition. Introduced and modernized by Ivan Schulman. Translated by Evelyn Picon Garfield. Detroit: Wayne State University Press, 1999.

Marquese, Rafael, Tamis Parron, and Marcia Berbel. *Slavery and Politics: Brazil and Cuba, 1790–1850*. Translated by Leonardo Marques. Albuquerque: University of New Mexico Press, 2016.

Marrero, Levi. *Cuba, economía y sociedad azúcar, ilustración y conciencia*. 15 vols. Ríos Piedras, PR: Editorial San Juan, 1972.

May, Bernard, ed. *Album pintoresco de la isla de Cuba*. Berlin and Havana: Bernard May & Co., Oilprinting Storch & Kramer, Libros Raros y Valiosos, BNJM, 1853.

Morant, Isabel, ed. and series coordinator. *Historia de las mujeres en España y América Latina. Del siglo XIX a los umbrales del XX*. Vol. 3. Madrid: Cátedra, 2006.

Moreno Fraginals, Manuel. *Cuba/España, España/Cuba. Una historia común*. Barcelona: Crítica, Grijalbo Mondadori, 1995.

———. *El Ingenio. Complejo económico-social cubano del azúcar*. 3 vols. Havana: Editorial de Ciencias Sociales, 1978.

Ortiz, Fernando. *Los Negros esclavos*. Havana: Editorial de Ciencias Sociales, 1996.

Paquette, Robert L. *Sugar Is Made with Blood: The Conspiracy of La Escalera and the Conflict between Empires over Slavery in Cuba*. Middletown, CT: Wesleyan University Press, 1988.

Perera Díaz, Aisnara, and María de los Angeles Meriño Fuentes, eds. *Estrategias de libertad: Un Acercamiento a las acciones legales de los esclavos en Cuba (1762–1872)*. 2 vols. Havana: Editorial de Ciencias Sociales, 2015.

Pérez, Louis A., Jr. *Intimations of Modernity: Civil Culture in Nineteenth-Century Cuba*. Chapel Hill: University of North Carolina Press, 2017.

Pérez de la Riva, Francisco. *El Café. Historia de su cultivo y explotación en Cuba*. Havana: Jesús Montero Editor, 1944.

Pichardo, Hortensia, ed. *Documentos para la historia de Cuba*. 5 vols. Havana: Editorial de Ciencias Sociales, 1968–80.

Piqueras, José Antonio. *La Esclavitud en las Españas. Un lazo trasatlántico*. 2d ed. Madrid: Catarata, 2017.

Pirala, Antonio. *Anales de la Guerra de Cuba*. Madrid: Felipe Fernández Rojas, 1895.

Piron, Hippolyte. *La Isla de Cuba (L'Ile de Cuba)*. Introduction by Olga Portuondo. Translated by Walfrido Díaz. Santiago de Cuba: Ediciones Santiago, 2015.

Portuondo, Fernando. *Estudios de historia de Cuba*. Havana: Editorial de Ciencias Sociales, 1986.

Portuondo Zuñiga, Olga. *Entre esclavos y libres de Cuba colonial*. Santiago de Cuba: Editorial Oriente, 2014.

———. "El Paraíso de Luisa Girard de Heredia." *Revista del Caribe* 61 (2014): 10–27.

Prados-Torreira, Teresa. *Mambisas: Rebel Women in Nineteenth-Century Cuba*. Gainesville: University Press of Florida, 2005.

Reid-Vázquez, Michele. *The Year of the Lash: Free People of Color in Cuba and the Nineteenth-Century Atlantic World*. Athens: University Press of Georgia, 2011.

Saco, José Antonio. *Historia de la esclavitud desde los tiempos más remotos hasta nuestros días*. 3 vols. 1875–78. Vols. 1 and 2: Paris: Imprenta Kugelman, 1875. Vol. 3: Barcelona: Imprenta de J. Jepus, 1878.

Salas y Quiroga, Jacinto. *Viajes de D. Jacinto de Salas y Quiroga*. 1840. Havana: Consejo Nacional de Cultura, 1964.

Santa Cruz y Montalvo, Mercedes, Condesa de Merlín. *Viaje a la Habana*. Havana: Editorial de Arte y Literatura, 1974.

Sartorius, David. *Ever Faithful: Race, Loyalty, and the Ends of Empire in Spanish Cuba*. Durham, NC: Duke University Press, 2013.

Schmidt-Nowara, Christopher. *Empire and Antislavery*. Pittsburgh: University of Pittsburgh Press, 1999.

Schwartz, Stuart B., ed. *Tropical Babylons: Sugar and the Making of the Atlantic World, 1450–1680*. Chapel Hill: University of North Carolina Press, 2004.

Scott, Rebecca J. "A Cuban Connection: Edwin F. Atkins, Charles Francis Adams, Jr., and the Former Slaves of Soledad Plantation." *Massachusetts Historical Review* 9 (2007): 7–34.

———. *Slave Emancipation in Cuba: The Transition to Free Labor*. Pittsburgh: University of Pittsburgh Press, 1985, 2000.

Singleton, Theresa A. *Slavery behind the Wall: An Archaeology of a Cuban Coffee Plantation*. Gainesville: University Press of Florida, 2015.

Steele, James W. *Cuban Sketches*. 1881. New York: G. P. Putnam's Sons, Knickerbocker Press, 1892.

Stoler, Ann. *Along the Archival Grain: Epistemic Anxieties and Colonial Common Sense*. Princeton, NJ: Princeton University Press, 2009.

Suárez y Romero, Anselmo. *Colección de artículos*. Havana: Establecimiento Tipográfico La Antilla, 1859.

———. *Francisco, el ingenio o las delicias del campo*. 1880. Havana: Ministerio de Educación, Dirección de Cultura, 1947.

Tanco Bosmeniel, Félix. *Petrona y Rosalía*. In *Cuentos cubanos del siglo XIX. Antología*, ed. Salvador Bueno, 103–31. Havana: Editorial Arte y Literatura, 1975.

Tomich, Dale. "'The Second Slavery': Bonded Labor and the Transformation of the Nineteenth-Century World Economy." In *Rethinking the Nineteenth Century*, ed. Francisco Ramírez, 103–17. Stanford, CA: Stanford University Press, 1998.

Torres Elers, Damaris. *María Cabrales, una mujer con historia propia*. Santiago de Cuba: Editorial Oriente, 2005.

Triay, José E. "El Calesero." In *Tipos y costumbres artículos de la isla de Cuba. Colección de por los mejores autores de este género. Obra ilustrada por D. Víctor Patricio Landaluze*. Havana: Editor Miguel Villa, 1881. Colección Facsimil, Libros Raros y Valiosos, 2010.

Trouillot, Michel-Rolph. *Silencing the Past: Power and Production of History*. Boston: Beacon Press, 1995.

Van Norman, William C., Jr. *Shade-Grown Slavery: The Lives of Slaves on Coffee Plantations in Cuba*. Nashville: Vanderbilt University Press, 2013.

Villaverde, Cirilo. *Cecilia Valdes or El Angel Hill*. 1882. Translated by Helen Lane. Ed. Sybille Fischer. Oxford: Oxford University Press, 2005.

Vinat Mata, Raquel. "Colores y dolores de la educación femenina en Cuba. Siglo XIX." In *Emergiendo del silencio: Mujeres Negras en la Historia de Cuba*, ed. Oilda Hevia Lanier and Daisy Rubiera Castillo, 89–129. Havana: Editorial de Ciencias Sociales, 2016.

Williams, Eric. *Capitalism and Slavery*. New York: Capricorn Books, 1944, 1966.

Williams, Lorna Valerie. *The Representation of Slavery in Cuban Fiction*. Columbia: University of Missouri Press, 1994.

Woodward, C. Vann, ed. *Mary Chesnut's Civil War*. New Haven, CT: Yale University Press, 1981.

Zambrana, Antonio. *El Negro Francisco. Novela de costumbres cubanas*. 1873. New ed. Havana: Imprenta P. Fernández y Cia., 1953.

Unpublished Sources

Fajardo, Sajay. "La Familia Stable Bonne. Su inserción en la actividad económica de Santiago de Cuba (1806–1868)." MA thesis, Universidad de Oriente, Santiago de Cuba, 2013.

O'Toole, Rachel. "Slavery, Freedom, and Intimate Obedience in Colonial Peru." Rethinking Freedom and Manumission in Latin America and the Atlantic World. AHA Conference, Chicago, January 3, 2019.

Suárez y Romero, Anselmo. "La Llegada al ingenio." 1863. BNJM, CM Suarez R. T. 6, no. 28, 268–70.

Websites

Lora Alvarez, Marta E. "Los Antiguos cafetales francohaitianos. Paisaje arqueológico de la humanidad." http://www.revistasexcelencias.com/excelencias-turisticas-cuba/santiago-amor-y-combate/dossier-unesco/los-antiguos-cafetales-francohait. Accessed August 25, 2019.

Voyages: The Translatlantic Slave Trade database. http://www.slavevoyages.org. Accessed August 25, 2019.

Index

Page numbers in italics indicate figures.